P9-CJH-464

Classic
RICE DISHES

Classic
RICE DISHES

Over 100 recipes from around the world

EDITED BY JANET SWARBRICK

CHARTWELL
BOOKS, INC.

A QUINTET BOOK

Published by Chartwell Books
A Division of Book Sales, Inc.
114 Northfield Avenue
Edison, New Jersey 08837

This edition produced for sale in the U.S.A., its territories
and dependencies only.

Copyright © 1996 Quintet Publishing Limited.
All rights reserved. No part of this publication may be
reproduced, stored in a retrieval system or transmitted in
any form or by any means, electronic, mechanical,
photocopying, recording or otherwise, without the
permission of the copyright holder.

ISBN 0-7858-0365-3

This book was designed and produced by
Quintet Publishing Limited
6 Blundell Street
London N7 9BH

Creative Director: Richard Dewing
Designer: Ian Hunt
Project Editor: Alison Bravington
Editor: Janet Swarbrick
Illustrator: Amanda Green

The material in this publication previously
appeared in: *Cajun Cooking* by Marjie Lambert,
Caribbean Cooking by Devinia Sookia, *The
Complete Rice Cookbook* by Myra Street, *The
Chicken Cookbook* by Wendy Veale, *Creole
Cooking* by Sue Mullin, *Lebanese Cooking* by Susan
Ward, *Mexican Cooking* by Roger Hicks, *Meze
Cooking* by Sarah Maxwell, *New Jewish Cooking* by
Elizabeth Wolf Cohen, *Nuevo Cubano Cooking* by
Sue Mullin, *Recipes from a Polish Kitchen* by
Bridget Jones, *Portuguese Cooking* by Hilaire
Walden, *Russian Regional Recipes* by Susan Ward,
Salsa Cooking by Marjie Lambert, *Scandinavian
Cooking* by Sonya Maxwell, *Southern Cooking* by
Marjie Lambert, *Spanish Cooking* by Pepita Aris,
Stir Fry Cooking by Bridget Jones, *Thai Cooking* by
Kurt Kahrs and *Vietnamese Cooking* by Paulette
Do Van.

Typeset in Great Britain by
Central Southern Typesetters, Eastbourne
Manufactured in Singapore by Eray Scan Pte Ltd
Printed in Singapore by
Star Standard Industries (Pte) Ltd

Contents

○ ○ ○

Introduction

∘ ∘ ∘

*R*ice is one of the oldest foods known to man, and forms the staple diet for well over half the human race. It is therefore undeniably the world's most important food. There are around 40,000 different varieties of rice grains, and it is not surprisingly one of the most versatile of the cereal crops.

Rice was cultivated in China as far back as 5,000 BC and may originally have been found wild in the foothills of the Himalayas. It took many centuries and the development of trade routes from the Far East to bring rice to Europe, where it first emerged as a popular and widely known food around the 17th century. Now internationally popular, rice features in the cooking of Spain, Italy, Portugal, and South America as well as the oriental countries. Rice is an essential buffer food with many spicy Chinese, Indian, and oriental dishes.

As it requires little preparation and is so easily stored in the home, rice is the ideal food for busy cooks. There is no wastage — any leftover rice quickly becomes the base for a rice/vegetable dish, a rice salad, or with additions, a main meal. Many people cook double quantities for just this reason.

Rice is easy to digest, and the processed form which does not require washing, if cooked with the minimum liquid, retains most of the nutrients. For those who are still more health conscious, brown rice (see page 8) is the most nutritious of all.

Mastering the art of cooking rice well is straightforward if you follow instructions on packets and in recipes. Timing is crucial in cooking with rice. It is advisable to follow instructions carefully for the first few times that you cook rice, and to watch it carefully while it is cooking.

Rice is good to eat. It has at last lost its image of a super-starchy food, and can be sensibly included in calorie-controlled diets. It is a source of quick energy, it contains some protein and the important B vitamins, and, as the perfect foil for so many fish, meat, and vegetable dishes, it really deserves to be part of your weekly menu.

MAIN TYPES OF RICE

Rice is one of the easiest foods to cook, and yet many people find themselves with a glutinous mess at the end of the cooking time. This may have something to do with the many varieties available and the confusion arising over the specially processed types that are now on sale. It is advisable to read the label when buying rice in order to ensure that you have selected the correct grain for your purpose.

The main types of rice are: long-grain (Patna) rice; long-grain brown rice; basmati rice (all long-grain rice); Italian risotto rice; "Carolina" or short-grain rice (both short-grain rice); ground rice; rice flour; rice flakes; and wild rice.

LONG-GRAIN RICE

This is a white long-grain rice that has been milled to remove the husk, the germ, and most of the layers of bran. This milling process is known as polishing, and the rice grains emerge long and thin in shape with an opaque appearance.

It is still sometimes referred to as Patna rice after the district in northeast India where it originated, but is now more often simply called long-grain rice as rice has not been exported from that part of India for many years. Most long-grain rice comes from the USA and Thailand; it is also grown in China, Australia, Guyana, India, Pakistan, and Burma.

Long-grain rice should be fluffy and light after cooking, and the grains should remain separate. It can be used to accompany stews, casseroles, curries, and vegetable dishes, and it is also a good addition to salads. Many spicy composite dishes such as Spanish paella and kedgeree, a baked fish casserole popular in England, are made up with fish, meat, or vegetables, using rice as the main ingredient.

LONG-GRAIN BROWN RICE

This is the long-grain rice which has been milled solely to remove the inedible husk. It used only to be sold in health food shops, but is now more widely available in supermarkets. This less-refined variety of rice retains some roughage, valuable B vitamins, minerals, and a small amount of protein.

Brown rice has a distinctly nutty flavor. It is less fluffy when cooked than other rices, and it has a slightly chewy texture in the mouth. It looks very similar to any other long-grain rice, but is a soft brown in color. There is no need to be alarmed if there is a slightly odd smell while cooking.

There are now several varieties of the easy-cook type available, and these usually have specific cooking instructions on the packet.

Note Brown rice usually takes longer to cook than white rice, but there are now several quick-cook varieties stocked in most supermarkets which will be ready after about 15 minutes.

Brown rice is excellent in salads, and can always be substituted for white rice.

BASMATI RICE

This is the name given to a long-grain rice which is grown in Pakistan and India. Basmati rice has a very distinctive taste and is excellent with oriental spicy dishes – as pilau rice or biriani. It is often said to be the prince of rices.

Basmati rice grains are slimmer than ordinary long-grain rice, and the color is a definite white. The grains are particularly light and fluffy when cooked, and basmati rice can be used in any recipe calling for long-grain rice. It is slightly more expensive, but the extra taste and texture are worth it.

ITALIAN RISOTTO RICE

This is a short-grain rice ideal for recipes in which liquids have to be absorbed, such as risotto dishes using any well-flavored stock. It is not necessary to wash this rice before use.

Risottos are cooked on top of the stove as the liquid has to be added gradually as the rice thickens – they have to be stirred and watched throughout the cooking time. Risottos commonly take their name from the town or area in Italy where they originated.

GROUND RICE

Ground rice is made by a prolongation of the milling process until the white rice becomes a little more granular than flour.

Ground rice is used for English milk puddings, which can be either boiled or baked, and is sometimes combined with flour for baked dishes.

CAROLINA OR SHORT-GRAIN RICE

Short-grain pudding rice has a round plump grain of chalky appearance. The name "Carolina" was given to pudding rice as it originally came from the southern states of that name. A lot of Carolina rice is now grown in China and Australia and exported.

The cooked grains are moist and tend to stick together, and are therefore perfect for a variety of dishes, including sweet dishes, desserts, sweet or spicy rissoles and croquettes.

RICE FLOUR

This is a fine flour milled from white rice which can be used in baked goods such as cakes and buns. It is sometimes used in rice desserts.

RICE FLAKES

This is a form of flaked rice, and is not widely used in Western-type cooking. It can be used in spicy dishes with pulses and functions generally as a thickening agent.

WILD RICE

This is not a true rice as the seeds come from a wild aquatic plant. It is an expensive food, and is often served with game and poultry. It requires long, slow cooking. The appearance is that of a long, grayish green seed.

Note There is now a product on sale which is a mixture of long-grain and wild rice. It makes a very interesting accompaniment for any spicy dish, and is excellent in salads.

CATERING QUANTITIES

○ **Long-grain rice**, **white**, **brown** and **basmati**, swells to about three times its original size when cooked.

Allow an average of ¼ cup uncooked rice per person if it is a side dish, or just a little less in mixed rice dishes with more than a pound of mixed vegetables, meat, or fish.

Allow ⅛ cup (about 3 tablespoons) per person for salads and spicy rices up to 12 people. For each additional person cook another 1–1½ tablespoons rice.

For rice salads as part of a buffet, 3 cups will be sufficient for 25 portions.

○ **Short-grain** rice is used for rice puddings. Allow ¼ cup uncooked rice to 2½ cups milk for 4 portions, or ⅓ cup rice to 3¾ cups milk for 6 portions.

○ For **yellow rice** saffron is traditionally used. It adds flavor and color to rice, but it is now so expensive that it has been widely replaced by yellow food coloring. For spicy dishes, turmeric may be added to give a good color, but this also flavors the rice slightly. Add the coloring to the boiling water and you will soon discover the right quantity for the shade of yellow required. Start by trying ¼–½ teaspoon turmeric or 6 drops yellow vegetable food coloring to each 2½ cups water.

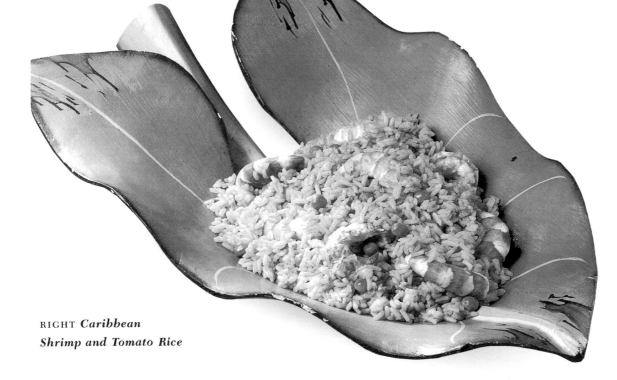

RIGHT *Caribbean Shrimp and Tomato Rice*

COOKING HINTS FOR RICE

❍ Be sure to read the label instructions carefully, and if you have easy-cook or parboiled rice follow the instructions given by the manufacturer.

❍ Wash only non-processed rice.

❍ If you are going to boil rice, use the correct amount of water or liquid and make sure it is boiling.

❍ Cover the rice tightly with a lid, and do not remove until the cooking time is almost up.

❍ Stir the rice only when it goes into the saucepan but not during the cooking, or it tends to become mushy.

❍ Do not leave the cooked rice in the cooking saucepan for longer than 10 minutes after it has cooked unless you want a large cake of stuck-together grains. Fork into a heated serving dish.

❍ For cooking rice in a microwave oven use the absorption method; that is, 2 measures of boiling water to 1 measure of rice. Cover with pierced plastic wrap, or a glass lid if using a microwave dish. Most long-grain rice

takes 20–25 minutes; basmati rice takes about 5 minutes less. The rice can be served directly from the microwave to the table.

It is advisable to check timings in your own microwave instruction book.

❍ Use a fork to fluff rice and not a spoon. A wooden fork is excellent – keep an old salad fork especially for this purpose.

❍ The easy-cook pre-fluffed varieties are slightly more expensive, but it is worth gaining confidence by trying these first. Always be sure to test the rice before the advised cooking time.

No kitchen cupboard is complete without several packets of rice. Quick meals can be conjured up in the event of the arrival of unexpected guests. Rice keeps well for long periods of time provided that it is kept dry. After a little experimentation, you will be surprised at the amazing variety of dishes which it can contribute to.

Starters, Side Dishes, and Salads

Fidellos Tostados

○ ○ ○

Spanish Sephardic Jews have been eating a very thin vermicelli-like pasta called fidellos for centuries. It is also popular in Greece, introduced by Spanish Jews when they fled Spain during the Inquisition. Cooks often break the pasta coils and throw in rice as in this recipe.

SERVES 6

12oz package vermicelli or angel hair pasta in coils
½ cup long-grain rice
2 tbsp olive oil
7oz can tomatoes, drained

2–3 cups chicken broth or water
1 tsp salt
½ tsp dried oregano
freshly ground black pepper
fresh coriander leaves

○ In a dry, large, heavy-bottomed frying pan, over medium–high heat, heat pasta and rice until golden brown, stirring frequently, 5–7 minutes. (It does not matter if pasta breaks a little.)

○ Add olive oil, tomatoes, chicken broth or water, salt, oregano, and black pepper to taste. Bring to a boil; reduce heat to medium and simmer, stirring often to unwind pasta, 7–10 minutes. Reduce heat to low, cover and cook 10 minutes longer until all the liquid is absorbed and pasta and rice are tender. Turn into a serving bowl and garnish with coriander leaves.

Curried Almond Rice

○ ○ ○

*C*ubans adore peas and rice. The Curry Butter Log in this recipe can be made in advance to complement rice dishes, shrimp or chicken, plain hot vegetables, and grilled tomatoes.

SERVES 4

*1 tbsp Curry Butter
  Log, softened*
3 cups water
1¼ cups rice

*1 cup frozen green
  peas, thawed and
  cooked (optional)*
*2 tbsp sliced almonds,
  toasted, if desired*

CURRY BUTTER LOG

*1 medium onion, finely
  chopped*
*1 cup butter, softened
  and divided in half*
2 tbsp curry powder

*4 tbsp prepared
  chutney, mashed
  with a fork*
*½ tsp freshly ground
  white pepper*

○ Make the Curry Butter Log first. In a small saucepan over moderately low heat, cook onion in half of the butter, stirring until softened. Stir in the curry powder, chutney, and white pepper. Let mixture cool.

○ In a bowl, cream together remaining butter and the curry mixture.

○ Reserve 1 tbsp of the mixture and transfer the rest of the mixture in the shape of a 12-inch log onto a piece of freezer paper or plastic wrap and roll up, twisting the ends of the paper in order to seal. Refrigerate until firm or freeze. Each yields about a dozen 1-tsp pats.

○ In an 8-inch frying pan, melt the reserved Curry Butter. Stir in water. Cover and heat to boiling. Stir in rice, reduce heat, cover and simmer about 12 minutes, or until rice is cooked. Add peas at end just long enough to heat. Sprinkle with almonds and serve.

Indian Rice with Tomatoes and Spinach

○ ○ ○

This is a mild, yet aromatic, rice dish from the Bene Israel Jewish community, near Bombay. Use fresh young spinach leaves if possible. Dhana jeera powder is a mixture of roasted and ground coriander and cumin seeds, available at ethnic grocery shops.

SERVES 6

3 tbsp vegetable oil
1 onion, cut in half and
    thinly sliced
1¾ cups basmati or
    long-grain rice,
    rinsed and soaked in
    cold water for 30
    minutes
10oz young spinach
    leaves, cooked and
    squeezed dry, or 10oz
    package frozen
    spinach, thawed and
    squeezed dry

2 medium tomatoes,
    peeled, seeded, and
    diced
¼ tsp turmeric
1 tsp dhana jeera
    powder (see above),
    or ¾ tsp ground
    coriander and ¼ tsp
    ground cumin
salt
freshly ground black
    pepper

○ In a large heavy saucepan, over medium–high heat, heat oil. Add onion and cook until softened and golden, 5–7 minutes. Drain rice well and add to onion. Cook, stirring constantly, until rice turns translucent and begins to color, 1–2 minutes.

○ Add spinach, tomatoes, turmeric, and dhana jeera powder or coriander and cumin. Add salt and pepper according to taste.

○ Pour in 2 cups water and stir. Bring rice mixture to a boil, then cover tightly and reduce heat to very low. Cook until water is completely absorbed and rice is tender, about 25 minutes.

○ Remove lid and fluff rice gently with a fork, being careful not to disturb the bottom layer, which will have formed a crust. Cover and cook 10 minutes longer. Spoon rice into a serving bowl; scrape up browned crisp crust from bottom and spoon around the rice. Serve hot.

Curried Wild Rice and Chicken Salad

○ ○ ○

The main components of this snappy Creole dish can be prepared ahead and combined at the last minute with the golden raisins, scallions, and nuts.

SERVES 6–8

4 cooked chicken
   breasts, chilled and
   cut into bite-sized
   pieces
1 bunch of scallions,
   chopped (including
   the green stem)

¾ cup golden raisins
½ cup slivered almonds
lettuce leaves, to
   garnish (optional)

DRESSING

2 cloves garlic,
   chopped
3 tbsp white wine
   vinegar
4 tbsp fresh lime juice
1½ tbsp curry powder
3 tbsp mango chutney

salt and freshly ground
   black pepper
⅔ cup olive oil
¾ cup sour cream
3 tbsp water
2 tbsp finely chopped
   coriander

WILD RICE MIXTURE

4–5½ cups cooked wild
   rice, prepared
   according to package
   instructions

1 tbsp white wine
   vinegar
2 tbsp olive oil
salt and freshly ground
   black pepper

○ Make the dressing first. In a blender or food processor, combine the garlic, vinegar, lime juice, curry powder, chutney, and salt and pepper to taste until the mixture is smooth. With the motor running, add the oil in a stream, then the sour cream and water, adding additional water if necessary to reach the desired consistency. Transfer the dressing to a small bowl and stir in the coriander. Cover and chill in the refrigerator.

○ To make the rice mixture, place the cooked rice in a bowl, add the vinegar, oil, and salt and pepper, and toss vigorously. Cover and chill in the refrigerator.

○ Just before serving, toss together the wild rice mixture, the chicken, and the dressing. Mix in the scallions, raisins, and almonds, and serve on lettuce leaves if desired.

Spanish Stuffed Tomatoes

○ ○ ○

SERVES 4

4 large tomatoes
¼ cup long-grain rice,
  cooked
salt and freshly ground
  pepper
2 tbsp oil
1 large onion, peeled
1 green pepper, seeded
  and sliced
1 chili pepper, seeded
  and sliced

½ tsp curry powder
  (optional)
¼ cup almonds,
  chopped
1 tsp chopped
  coriander or chopped
  parsley
2oz (about ½ cup)
  cooked ground beef,
  lamb, or chicken

○ Remove the top of the tomatoes. Scoop out the centers into a bowl.

○ Add the cooked long-grain rice. Season well.

○ Heat the oil and fry the onion over a low heat for 3 minutes. Add the sliced pepper and chili. Sprinkle with the curry powder and continue cooking for 2 minutes. Add the chopped almonds.

○ Finally, sprinkle in the chopped coriander or parsley. Add the meat and mix well.

○ Fill each tomato with the rice mixture. Brush the tomatoes with oil, and cook in the oven at 350°F for about 15 minutes.

LEFT *Spanish Stuffed Tomatoes*

Gingery Jasmine Rice

o o o

Use the finest rice you can find for this Cuban dish, and the result will be a creamy, risotto-like texture. You can add bits of leftover meat, fish, or seafood to this for a one-dish meal. The Pineapple Butter can be used as dip for barbecued lobster, shrimp, or scallops.

SERVES 4

1¼ cups jasmine or
   basmati rice
¼ tsp ground cumin
1 tsp Pineapple Butter
   Log

1 cup water
1 tsp grated fresh
   ginger root

PINEAPPLE BUTTER LOG

1 cup butter,
   softened

¼ cup canned
   pineapple, drained
   and finely chopped

O To make the Butter Log, beat the ingredients in a small bowl. Reserve 1 tsp and transfer rest of mixture in the shape of a 12-inch log onto a piece of freezer paper or plastic wrap. Roll up, twisting the ends of the paper to seal. Refrigerate to firm or freeze.

O Rinse rice in cold water several times until water runs clear, then drain.

O In a medium saucepan, sauté cumin in Butter Log, about 30 seconds. Stir in rice, water, and ginger. Bring to a boil, then cover, reduce heat to very low, and cook 12 minutes without lifting the lid.

O Remove pan from the heat and let sit, covered, for at least 5 and up to 20 minutes. Before serving, fluff rice well with a fork.

Pineapple Rice

○   ○   ○

This "show-off" dish is quite easy to make but always impressive to present. Although the pineapple also adds flavor to the rice, there is scarcely any point attempting it just with pineapple pieces — appearance is everything.

SERVES 4–6

1 pineapple
4 tbsp peanut or corn
   oil
3½ cups cooked rice
¼ lb (about ¾ cup)
   finely diced ham
½ tbsp chopped garlic
⅓ cup raisins

2 tbsp chicken broth
2 tsp curry powder
1 tsp sugar
1 tsp salt
¼ tsp ground white
   pepper

○ Cut one side off the pineapple lengthwise to expose the inside. Carefully remove the inside fruit and cut into small dice. Reserve the outside of the pineapple.

○ Heat the oil in a pan or wok, add the ham and garlic, stir-fry, then add ½ cup of the diced pineapple (save the remainder for use in another dish) and all the rest of the ingredients. Mix well. Spoon into the empty pineapple, cover with the pineapple lid, and bake in a preheated 275°F oven for 30 minutes.

19

Pine Nuts
and Currants with Rice

o o o

*P*ilau rice has infiltrated from India and Iran and from Turkey. This simple version is often served molded to accompany a main course.

SERVES 4

⅓ cup olive oil
2 small onions, finely chopped
4 tbsp pine nuts
2 tbsp currants
½ tsp saffron threads

2 cups long-grain rice
salt and freshly ground pepper
fresh parsley and coriander
paprika

O Heat the olive oil over medium heat and sauté the chopped onions until they are limp — about 6–8 minutes. Add the pine nuts and sauté for a few minutes more, until both the onions and nuts are lightly colored. Stir in the currants, saffron, and rice, and cook for about 1 minute or until the rice is just transparent.

O Add salt to taste and pour in water to cover, about 3 cups. Cook, covered, on high heat until the water begins to be absorbed, then turn the heat off and allow it to sit for about 20 minutes, or until all the water is absorbed and the rice tender. If it is still not tender, add a tablespoon or so more water and simmer for a couple of minutes. Then leave to sit for a further 5 minutes.

O If desired, press the cooked rice into a mold(s) before turning out onto a plate garnished with parsley and coriander. Dust the rice with paprika.

Trinity Rice
with Almonds

o o o

*M*ade with onions, peppers, and celery — the Holy Trinity of Cajun cooking — this Louisiana version of a side dish of rice pilaf has the added bonus of almonds.

SERVES 8

2 tbsp butter or olive oil
1 stalk celery, chopped
1 small green pepper, chopped
1 medium onion, chopped
2 cloves garlic, finely chopped
⅓ cup blanched almonds, slivered or sliced

1 tsp Worcestershire sauce
1½ tsp salt
¼ tsp black pepper
1 tomato, seeded and chopped
4–5 scallions, chopped
2 tbsp chopped fresh parsley
1 cup white rice

O In a medium frying pan, heat the butter or olive oil. Sauté the celery, green pepper, onion, and garlic until limp, about 5 minutes.

O Remove the vegetables and set aside. If there is no oil left in pan, add about 1 tbsp more.

O Add the almonds, and stir until lightly browned. Add the Worcestershire sauce and stir well. Set aside.

O In a large saucepan, bring 3 cups water to the boil. Add the salt, pepper, tomato, scallions, parsley, sautéed vegetables, and almonds and return to the boil. Add the rice, stir well, and reduce the heat to very low; cover and cook until all the water is absorbed, 20–25 minutes. Or, to avoid scorching, turn off the burner and let rice cook in its own steam for the last few minutes.

RIGHT *Trinity Rice with Almonds*

Pistachios and Rice Salad

o   o   o

This salad comes from Iran and the eastern borders of Lebanon. It is exceptionally delicious made with 4 tbsp pistachio oil substituted for the olive oil used to toss the salad. This can be obtained in delicatessens, but is unfortunately very expensive.

SERVES 6

1½ cups long-grain rice
5 tbsp olive oil
salt and freshly ground pepper
3 tbsp fresh lemon juice
1 tsp grated lemon peel
1 tsp pomegranate seeds

3 tbsp finely chopped flat-leaved parsley
4 scallions, finely chopped
½ cup shelled pistachios

O Sauté the rice in 1 tbsp olive oil, stirring to coat thoroughly. (If substituting pistachio oil for the dressing, sauté the rice in sunflower oil instead of olive oil.) When the rice is transparent, add salt to taste and boiling water to cover, bring to a boil, and cover. Reduce the heat for 5 minutes and simmer, then turn off the heat and let the rice sit until it has absorbed all the water and is tender — about 25 minutes. (If necessary, add a drop or two of boiling water if the rice is still not tender. Stir, and leave for another 5 minutes.) Put the rice aside in a serving bowl to dry and cool.

O In a small bowl, whisk together the lemon juice and the remaining olive oil (or pistachio oil). Season to taste, and add the lemon peel and pomegranate seeds. Set the mixture aside.

O To the bowl with the rice add the parsley, scallions, and pistachios. Stir in the lemon dressing. Cover and chill for at least 2 hours before serving.

Hoppin' John

o o o

This dish is undoubtedly African in origin. No one quite knows how it got its name, but each cook seems to have his or her own recipe for this mixture of rice and black-eyed peas. Folklore holds that eating it on New Year's Day brings good luck, probably because the dish is so filling you won't want for much more. Unfortunately, it also brings fat and cholesterol when cooked in the traditional manner with knuckle of bacon or pig cheeks. This adaptation will bring better nutrition as well as luck. If you wish to make a vegetarian version, just skip the meat altogether.

SERVES 4

3 cups water
2 chicken stock cubes
1 medium ripe tomato, chopped
10 scallions, chopped
1 bay leaf
1 tsp dried thyme
1 tsp hot pepper or Tabasco sauce
1¼ cups long-grain white rice
1 x 1lb can black-eyed peas, drained and rinsed
6oz (approx 1½ cups) cooked ham, trimmed of fat and cut in cubes
salt and freshly ground black pepper

○ Bring the water, stock cubes, tomato, scallions, bay leaf, thyme, and hot pepper sauce to the boil in a large saucepan.

○ Add the rice, cover, and simmer until tender, about 25 minutes.

○ Stir in the black-eyed peas and ham, cover, and simmer for 8–10 minutes.

Pigeon Peas and Rice

o o o

This dish is eaten on many of the Caribbean islands. If you can't find pigeon peas, substitute red beans, preferably small red kidney beans. This dish is great with chicken or any meat, and can make a one-dish meal if leftover bits of meat are added.

SERVES 4

2 tbsp oil
1 small onion, chopped
2 cloves garlic, crushed
4 tbsp tomato paste
2 ripe tomatoes, chopped
1 green sweet pepper, chopped
½ tsp thyme
4 tbsp chopped fresh coriander

1 x 1lb can pigeon peas, drained
scant 1 cup long-grain white rice
2 cups water
2 tbsp fresh lime juice
hot pepper or Tabasco sauce to taste
salt and freshly ground black pepper to taste

○ Heat the oil in a saucepan and add the onion. Cook gently for 5 minutes, then add the garlic and tomato paste, chopped ripe tomatoes, green sweet peppers, and thyme. Cook for another minute.

○ Add the coriander, pigeon peas, and rice, and sauté for 1 minute.

○ Add the water and lime juice and cook gently, covered, for 15 minutes until the rice is cooked.

○ Add hot pepper or Tabasco sauce, salt and pepper to taste, and serve.

Herbed Rice Cakes

o   o   o

A variation on an old favorite, rice croquettes, these herbed cakes were popularized in Miami by Yuca, the Nuevo Cubano restaurant. Garnish with a dollop of sour cream sprinkled with some of the chives. These are great as an alternate to potatoes with almost any entrée.

O   Combine rice, egg, onion, 4 tsp parsley, tomato, chives, and thyme. Pat into 6 large or 12 small patties.

O   In a heavy-bottomed frying pan over medium–high heat, fry rice cakes, turning once, until golden brown, on both sides. Cook in batches if necessary. Drain on paper towels, garnish with rest of parsley, and serve immediately.

SERVES 4–6

2 cups cooked rice
1 egg, lightly beaten
1 small onion, finely chopped
2 tbsp finely chopped fresh parsley
1 tomato, finely chopped

1 bunch chives, finely chopped
1 bunch thyme, finely chopped
1–2 tbsp olive oil for frying
4 tbsp sour cream for garnish (optional)

Lebanese Stuffed Vine Leaves

○ ○ ○

Stuffed vine leaves are popular all over the eastern Mediterranean crescent, from Greece to Egypt. Unlike some other nationalities, however, the Lebanese prefer their stuffing without meat and served cold.

MAKES ABOUT 25

1 x 6oz package vine leaves (about 35)	salt and pepper
4 tbsp olive oil	1 tbsp raisins or currants
1 large onion, finely chopped	1½ tbsp finely chopped mint
2 tbsp pine nuts	½ tbsp cinnamon
¼ cup long-grain rice	juice of 2 lemons

○ Remove the vine leaves from the package, separate them, place in a large container, and pour boiling water over them. Allow to soak for 15 minutes, then drain. Return to the bowl, pour cold water on them, soak for a further 10 minutes, then drain thoroughly on paper towels.

○ Heat 1 tbsp of the olive oil in a large frying pan. Add the pine nuts and sauté, stirring, for about 4 minutes, or until the nuts are golden. Remove the pine nuts with a slotted spoon and reserve. Add another 1 tbsp of oil to the pan, and stir in the onions. Sauté until limp and lightly colored, about 5–6 minutes, then add the rice and

salt to taste. Stir the rice until it is coated with the oil, then pour in ½ cup boiling water to cover. Reduce the heat, cover, and cook over medium heat for about 5 minutes. Take off the heat and allow to sit until the water has been absorbed, and the rice is tender — about 20 minutes. Stir in the raisins or currants, pine nuts, chopped mint, and cinnamon.

○ Lay a vine leaf flat, and spoon 2 tbsp of the rice mixture near the stem end. Roll the leaf one turn over the mixture, then tuck in the sides of the leaf toward the center. Continue to roll the leaf like a cigar, until you reach the end. Squeeze the bundle to remove excess moisture. Repeat the process with the remaining leaves and stuffing.

○ If there are any vine leaves left over, lay them on the bottom of a lightly oiled casserole. Arrange the stuffed leaves in a single layer on top. Pour the lemon juice over the top and just enough hot water to cover. Drizzle over the remaining 2 tbsp olive oil. Weigh the stuffed leaves down with a plate. Cover tightly and cook over high heat for about 4 minutes, then lower the heat and simmer for about 40 minutes. Remove from the heat, uncover, and allow to cool in the cooking liquid. When cold, remove the stuffed leaves with a slotted spoon and arrange on a platter.

○ Serve at room temperature or chilled, together with lemon wedges.

Creole Black Beans and Rice Salad

○ ○ ○

*I*f you have some leftover cooked rice on hand, this dish can be whipped up in just a few minutes. For color, lay strips of pimento or red sweet pepper across the top of the dish.

SERVES 4–6

1¼ lb canned black
  beans, rinsed and
  drained
2 cups cooked rice
½ cup fresh coriander
¼ cup lime juice
¾ cup oil

1 small onion, chopped
2 cloves garlic, crushed
salt and freshly ground
  black pepper
pimento or red sweet
  pepper strips
  (optional)

○ Mix the beans, rice, and coriander together in a bowl.

○ Place the lime juice in a small bowl and whisk in the oil. Add the onion and garlic, and toss with the beans.

○ Add salt and pepper to taste, and garnish with pimento or red sweet pepper. This dish can either be served at room temperature or chilled.

Dirty Rice

o o o

Dirty rice is a traditional Cajun dish served as a main course or side dish. You may substitute the gizzard cooking water for part of the chicken stock. This recipe is baseline spicy — the Cajuns eat it hotter — so taste and adjust seasonings accordingly.

SERVES 6

½ lb chicken gizzards, or a combination of hearts and gizzards
2 tbsp vegetable oil
1 onion, chopped
1 stalk celery, chopped
½ green pepper, chopped
3 cloves garlic, finely chopped
2oz chicken livers, trimmed and chopped

2oz ground pork (not sausage)
1 cup chicken stock or canned broth
¼ tsp black pepper
¼ tsp salt
¼ tsp cayenne
½ tsp dry mustard
½ tsp ground cumin
1⅓ cups cooked white rice
2 scallions, chopped
2 tbsp chopped fresh parsley

O Put the gizzards in a small saucepan, cover with water, and bring to the boil. Reduce the heat and simmer, uncovered, for 1 hour, adding extra water if necessary. Drain the gizzards. Set aside until cool enough to chop.

O In a large saucepan over medium heat, heat the oil. Sauté the onions, celery, green pepper, and garlic for about 5 minutes. Add the livers and pork and cook, stirring, until meat is browned. Add the chopped gizzards, chicken stock, and spices, and continue cooking until the liquids are slightly reduced. Taste and adjust seasonings.

O If the rice was not cooked with salt, add more salt here. Add the rice, scallions, and parsley, and cook just until heated through, about 2 minutes.

Fried Rice with Fish Sauce

o o o

This is a spicy and traditional version of Thai fried rice. The spicy sauce is found on all Thai tables, and is used to add both spiciness and saltiness to dishes.

SERVES 4–6

2 tbsp peanut or corn oil

5 cups cooked rice
3 tbsp Fish Sauce

FISH SAUCE

¼ cup Thai fish sauce
10 fresh small green chilies, sliced into small circles

1 tsp sliced shallot
¼ tsp palm sugar
1 tbsp lime or lemon juice

O To make the Fish Sauce just mix all the ingredients together well.

O Stir-fry the rice in the oil for 1 minute, add the sauce, mix well, and cook for 1 more minute. Remove from the heat.

O Serve accompanied by preserved salted eggs, cucumber slices, fried eggs, and raw vegetables.

BELOW **Fried Rice with Fish Sauce**

29

Hot and Spicy
Mexican Green Rice

○ ○ ○

This spicy rice dish is flavored with coriander and Roast Jalapeño Salsa. Try this salsa on biscuits, over steamed vegetables, or on meat or fish.

SERVES 6–8

½ cup Roast Jalapeño Salsa	3 cups chicken broth
small handful fresh coriander	3 tbsp vegetable oil
	1¾ cups white rice
small handful fresh parsley	1½ tsp salt

ROAST JALAPEÑO SALSA
MAKES ABOUT ¾ CUP

15 jalapeño chilies	¼ tsp dried oregano
4 Anaheim chilies	2 tbsp olive oil
½in thick slices of red onion, peeled	1 tbsp fresh lemon juice
5 cloves garlic, unpeeled	¼ tsp salt

○ To make the Salsa, cut the jalapeños and Anaheims in half, and remove the seeds and veins. Cook the chilies, onion slices, and garlic in the broiler, remembering to keep the skins of the chilies facing the heat source. The chilies will cook unevenly, and it's not necessary for the skins to be completely blackened. Don't cook them until they are charred through to the flesh. Remove them from the heat when they are ready, and seal in a plastic bag or foil pouch. Leave them in the bag or pouch for 10 minutes. This will loosen the skins and make them easier to remove.

○ The onion slices should soften and brown slightly. Turn and cook them on both sides. Turn the garlic once and cook until cloves are softened. Garlic will turn bitter if it is charred, so watch it closely.

○ With a sharp knife, peel and scrape the skins off the chilies. Jalapeño skins are not as tough as many other chilies, so it's all right to leave part of the skin on. Roast chilies have a tendency to get stringy, so cut them in strips from side to side, not lengthwise. Put the strips in a food processor.

○ Cut each onion slice into quarters and add them to the food processor. Peel the garlic, trim off any burnt spots, and add that, too. Add remaining ingredients, and process until they are well chopped but not a paste. The mixture will be fairly dry.

○ In a blender or food processor, purée the salsa, coriander, and parsley with about 1 cup chicken broth. Set aside.

○ Heat the oil in a frying pan. Add the rice and cook, stirring frequently, 10 minutes. If the pan does not have at least a 2-quart capacity, transfer the rice to a large pan. Add the purée, the remaining broth, and the salt. Bring to the boil, cover, and reduce the heat. Cook until the liquid has been absorbed and the rice is tender, 20–25 minutes. Fluff the rice with a fork and let stand covered for another 5 minutes before serving.

BELOW *Hot and Spicy Mexican Green Rice*

Spicy Rice Stuffing with Greens

o o o

This Southern rice dish was designed as a stuffing, but you can serve it as a side dish, too. The almonds add crunch, and the greens add a subtle flavor. This recipe calls for mustard greens, but you can substitute another type of greens if your prefer.

MAKES ABOUT 5 CUPS STUFFING

½ lb cleaned and chopped mustard greens
2–4 tbsp vegetable oil
1 medium onion, chopped
½ celery stalk, chopped
⅓ cup chopped green pepper
2 garlic cloves, finely chopped

1 cup chicken broth
¼ tsp black pepper
¼ tsp salt
¼ tsp cayenne
½ tsp dry mustard
¼ tsp ground cumin
⅓ cup flaked almonds, toasted (see note)
2⅔ cups cooked rice
2 scallions, chopped

O Wash the mustard greens at least twice. Run enough water into the sink to cover the greens. Swish the greens through the water, lift them out, and drain the water. Then rinse any grit from the sink, refill with fresh water and clean again, until all the grit has been washed out. Dry the greens with absorbent paper towels or in a salad spinner. Cut out and discard the coarse part of the stalk. Chop the greens into 1-inch pieces. In a medium frying pan, sauté the greens in 2 tbsp vegetable oil until the greens are limp, 4–5 minutes. Remove the greens from the pan and set aside.

O Add oil to the pan if needed and sauté the onion, celery, green pepper, and garlic until they are tender, about 5 minutes. Add the chicken broth and spices. (If the rice was not cooked with salt, add another 1 tsp salt.) Cook over medium heat until the liquids are slightly reduced. Add the greens, almonds, rice, and scallions. Stir well. Any excess stuffing can be cooked 20 minutes, covered, in a lightly oiled casserole dish.

O Note: to toast almonds, spread in a single layer on baking sheet. Bake at 350°F until lightly browned, about 10 minutes. Be warned though — the almonds turn quickly from light brown to black.

Waldorf Rice Salad

o o o

SERVES 4

1 cup long-grain rice
1 small onion, peeled
  and finely chopped
6 stalks celery, washed
4 scallions washed and
  chopped

½ cup walnuts,
  chopped
1 red apple
1 green apple
⅔ cup mayonnaise
1 tbsp parsley
juice of 1 lemon

O Cook the rice until fluffy, forking from time to time to separate the grains. Allow to cool.

O Add the finely chopped onion to the rice and mix well.

O Remove the strings from the celery stalks and chop finely. Add to the rice.

O Add the chopped scallions and walnuts to the rice, and mix well.

O Chop part of both apples into small cubes, sprinkle with lemon juice, and mix with the rice salad, mayonnaise, and parsley.

Risotto Milanese

o o o

*T*his side dish from Italy can be garnished with mushrooms.

SERVES 4

1 tbsp olive oil
¼ cup butter
1 medium onion, peeled
  and finely chopped
1½ cups Italian risotto
  rice
3 cups hot chicken
  broth

⅔ cup white wine
salt and freshly ground
  pepper
1 tbsp freshly chopped
  parsley (optional)
⅓ cup grated Parmesan
  cheese

O Using a heavy-bottomed saucepan, heat the oil and 2 tbsp butter. Add the onion, and cook over a low heat for about 3–4 minutes without browning.

O Add the risotto rice dry, and stir fry for about 2 minutes over a medium heat.

O Add half the hot chicken broth. Stir from the bottom to avoid sticking, and continue to do so until the grains are separate and the broth is absorbed.

O Continue adding the remaining broth and white wine with 1 tsp salt bit by bit, stirring all the time, until it is all absorbed. The risotto should have cooked to a creamy consistency in about 25 minutes, without becoming mushy.

O Add 2 tbsp butter and the cheese at the end of the cooking time, just before serving.

O Add the freshly ground pepper and, if you wish, a little freshly chopped parsley for flavor.

LEFT **Waldorf Rice Salad**

RIGHT **Risotto Milanese**

Rice with Spinach

o o o

SERVES 4

scant 1 cup long-grain
  rice, cooked
4 tbsp oil
½ small onion, chopped
3 tbsp cumin seeds
1 tsp turmeric

knob of butter
  (optional)
½ lb fresh spinach,
  cooked, drained, and
  shredded

O The rice should be freshly cooked and drained if
necessary. If cooked by the absorption method, do not
fork up the grains but leave the pan covered off the heat
when the rice is cooked.

O Heat the oil and stir fry the onion with the cumin
seeds for 5 minutes. Stir in the turmeric and continue to
cook for 2 minutes before adding the butter, if used.
Allow the butter to melt, then add the rice and stir fry for
2 minutes until it has become well coated in the flavoring
ingredients.

O Make a well in the rice or push it to one side of the
pan and add the spinach. Stir fry the spinach briefly to
heat it through. Then fork the spinach into the rice and
serve at once.

Spiced Rice Salad

o   o   o

SERVES 4

1 cup rice
1 tsp salt
1 tsp garam masala
1 tsp turmeric
1 bay leaf
2 tbsp butter
1 clove garlic, crushed

1 onion, diced
⅓ cup golden raisins
1 green pepper, seeded,
    blanched, and diced
6 tbsp low-fat yogurt
2 scallions, washed and
    chopped

O Cook the rice in boiling salted water with the garam masala, turmeric, and bay leaf for about 15 minutes, until tender.

O Meanwhile, melt the butter and gently sweat the garlic and onion without browning for 5 minutes.

O Add the garlic and onion to the rice when it is cooked, and allow it to cool.

O Stir in the raisins and pepper.

O Garnish with chopped scallions. Stir in yogurt before serving.

Minestrone Soup

o o o

If you are making the broth for this soup, a ham bone gives an excellent flavor and any meat on the bone can be added to the pot.

SERVES 4–6

¼ cup butter
2 onions, peeled and finely chopped
2 carrots, scraped and diced
½ cup peas or sliced green beans
1 small turnip, peeled and diced
2 stalks of celery, washed
4½ cups water or broth
4 tbsp tomato paste

1 bay leaf
1 bouquet garni (see note)
½ tsp mixed herbs
¼ cup long-grain rice
2 leeks, washed and chopped
salt and freshly ground pepper
¼ small cabbage, finely shredded
1 tbsp chopped parsley
2 tbsp grated cheese

O Prepare all the vegetables.

O Melt the butter and toss the onion, celery, carrots, peas or beans, and turnip in the saucepan. Stir over a low heat for about 4 minutes.

O Add the water or broth to the vegetables. Then add the tomato paste, bouquet garni, bay leaf, and mixed herbs. Bring to the boil. Add rice and simmer for 15 minutes.

O Add leeks and seasoning and continue cooking for a further 5 minutes.

O Finally, add the finely shredded cabbage and cook for a further 5 minutes or until the rice is cooked. Toss in chopped parsley and serve with grated cheese on top.

Note: to make your own bouquet garni, place a bay leaf and a few sprigs of parsley and thyme in a small square of cheesecloth. Gather up the ends and tie tightly with string. Remove the bag before serving.

Tomato Rice

○ ○ ○

This is one of the most popular of the many Portuguese rice dishes. Much of its character comes from the well-flavored tomatoes, so choose them carefully, many supermarkets are now selling varieties that have been grown specifically for their flavor. If the rice is still soggy at the end of cooking, it is described as *malandrinho* (naughty). Serve the rice with roast, grilled or fried meat, poultry or fish, fish cakes, or omelets.

SERVES 4

2 tbsp olive oil
1 large onion, finely chopped
1 garlic clove, finely chopped
2 ripe, well-flavored tomatoes, skinned, seeded, and finely chopped

1 cup long-grain rice
2½ cups boiling water
2 tbsp chopped parsley
salt and pepper

○ Heat the oil in a saucepan, add the onion and garlic, and fry until softened but not brown.

○ Stir in the tomatoes, and cook for a further 5 minutes or so before adding the rice. Stir to coat with the vegetables, then add the boiling water. Bring to the boil, cover, and cook over a low heat until the rice is tender and all the liquid has been absorbed. Stir in the parsley and seasoning to taste.

Spanish Rice

o o o

This is a pleasantly spicy version of Spanish Rice often served with Mexican food. The spices are briefly fried to develop their flavor, then rice is added and fried. It is then steamed in water and salsa.

MAKES 6–8 SERVINGS

3 tbsp vegetable oil	1¾ cups white rice
1 tsp chili powder	1¼ cups Salsa
½ tsp ground cumin	1 tsp salt
½ tsp dried oregano	
2 cloves garlic, put through a garlic press	

SALSA

MAKES ABOUT 1¼ CUPS

3 large tomatoes	3 tbsp finely chopped coriander
1 small onion, finely chopped	1 tbsp olive oil
2 cloves garlic, finely chopped	1 tbsp lime juice
2 jalapeño chilies, seeded and chopped	salt to taste

O Heat the oil in a heavy frying pan. Add the chili powder, cumin, oregano, and garlic and cook for 1 minute, stirring constantly. If the oil is very hot, remove the pan from the heat and let the spices cook in the heat from the oil. After 1 minute, add the rice. Cook for 10 minutes, stirring almost constantly.

O To make the Salsa, core the tomatoes, cut them in half, and squeeze the seeds out. Place the tomatoes cut side down on a flameproof baking sheet and place them under the broiler. (*Note:* If the baking sheet does not have sides, line it with foil, then crimp the edges to form a shallow basin to catch the tomato juice.) Broil the tomatoes until the skin is just slightly blackened and loose. Slide off their skins, drain off excess juices, and let them cool.

O While the tomatoes are cooling, mix together all the remaining ingredients. Then chop the tomatoes and add them to the Salsa. Let stand for 15 minutes or so, then taste and adjust the seasoning.

O Transfer the seasoned rice to a large pan and add 2½ cups water, the Salsa, and salt. Bring to the boil, cover, and reduce the heat. Cook until the liquid has been absorbed and the rice is tender, 20–25 minutes. Fluff with a fork. Let stand, covered, for 5 minutes, then serve.

Stuffed Sweet Peppers

o o o

This, the New World version of *chiles rellenos* made with sweet peppers, rice and meat, is also popular in the Old World.

SERVES 4

3 strips of bacon, finely chopped	½ lb ground beef
1 tbsp olive oil	2 cups Spanish Rice
1 small onion, chopped	4 very large green sweet peppers

O Fry the bacon in a little oil; in the bacon fat, fry the onion and beef. When the beef is cooked, add the rice. Warm through.

O Cut the tops off the peppers. Remove the seeds and veins. Stuff the beef-bacon-rice mixture into the peppers. (Let it mound over the top if necessary.) Bake in a moderately hot oven at 400°F until the peppers are cooked — about 30–40 minutes.

RIGHT **Spanish Rice**

Chicken and Wild Rice Salad

o o o

SERVES 4

¾ cup long-grain and
  wild rice, cooked
½ lb (about 2 cups)
  cooked chicken,
  chopped
1 small onion, peeled
⅓ cup well-flavored
  mayonnaise

¼ lb mushrooms,
  washed
1 tbsp lemon juice
4 tbsp canned corn
7 black olives, sliced
salt and freshly ground
  pepper
1 head lettuce
2 heads chicory

O Cook the rice as directed on the package of mixed long-grain and wild rice. Allow to cool.

O Add the chopped chicken to the cooled rice.

O Chop the onion finely and add to the mixture along with the mayonnaise.

O Slice the mushrooms thinly. Mix with the rice, retaining a few for the top of the salad. Pour the lemon juice over the retained mushrooms. Add the corn and 4 sliced olives to the mixture and season.

O Arrange the lettuce and sliced chicory in the salad bowl. Turn the chicken and rice mixture into the bowl. Garnish with the mushroom slices and the remaining black olives.

Thai Rice Salad

o o o

*T*his is another "leftover" dish made with rice from a previous occasion — the southern version.

SERVES 4–6

2 cups cooked rice
1¾ cups unsweetened
  grated fresh coconut,
  browned in a 350°F
  oven for 5–8 minutes
1 small pomelo or
  grapefruit, shredded
½ cup dried shrimp,
  chopped

½ cup bean sprouts
¼ cup finely sliced
  lemon grass
10 sliced green (string)
  beans
2 dried red chilies,
  pounded
1 tbsp finely shredded
  kaffir lime leaf

SAUCE

1 cup water
2 tbsp chopped
  anchovies
1 tbsp palm sugar

2 kaffir lime leaves,
  torn into small pieces
¼ tsp sliced lemon
  grass

O Put all the sauce ingredients in a pan, boil for 5 minutes, remove from the heat, and strain. Put to one side.

O Place the rice in half-cup molds or large ramekins, press, and invert onto a large serving platter. Arrange the rest of the raw ingredients around the edge of the rice in separate piles.

O To eat, spoon some rice onto individual plates, and take a little of each ingredient to mix with the rice according to taste. Spoon the sauce over the top.

LEFT **Chicken and Wild Rice Salad**

Egg, Cheese, and Vegetable Main Dishes

Cajun Red Beans and Rice

o o o

Serve this flavorful, slow-cooked dish with the Salsa and sour cream. Extra vegetables are added near the end of the cooking time.

SERVES 6–8

1 x 1lb package dry kidney beans, picked over
3 tbsp olive oil
1 large onion, chopped
4 garlic cloves, finely chopped
2 stalks celery, chopped
1 carrot, chopped
1 green pepper, seeded and chopped
1 tbsp salt
¼ tsp cayenne pepper
¼ tsp white pepper
¼ tsp black pepper

1 tsp dried thyme
1½ tsp ground cumin
1 tsp dry mustard
1 bay leaf
1 x 6oz can tomato paste
½ cup dry red wine
few drops of Tabasco sauce
1 stalk celery, chopped
½ green pepper, chopped
4 scallions, chopped
3–3½ cups cooked rice to serve
sour cream

SALSA

2 large tomatoes, seeded and chopped
4 scallions, chopped
½ long mild chili, such as Anaheim or poblano

1 tbsp fresh chopped parsley
1 tbsp white wine vinegar
1 tbsp olive oil
few drops Tabasco, to taste

○ In 1 gallon water, soak the beans at least 4 hours or overnight. Drain, rinse and return to the large pot with 5 cups water. Bring to the boil, then reduce the heat and simmer, skimming the foam, while you prepare the vegetables.

○ In a frying pan, heat the oil and sauté the onion, garlic, 2 chopped stalks celery, carrot and 1 chopped green pepper, until wilted, about 5 minutes. Add the vegetables to the beans, along with the seasonings, tomato paste and wine and continue simmering, stirring occasionally, until cooked.

○ To make the Salsa, mix all the Salsa ingredients together. Serve it with sour cream, along with the Red Bean and Rice dish.

Savory Rice Ring with Vegetable Curry

o   o   o

SERVES 4

RICE RING

1 cup basmati or long-
  grain rice
3 tbsp oil
1 onion, peeled and
  finely chopped
¼ green pepper, washed
  and seeded

1 red pepper, washed
  and seeded
salt and freshly ground
  pepper
¼ tsp garam masala

VEGETABLE CURRY

1 large onion, peeled
1 clove garlic, crushed
1-inch piece fresh
  ginger root
1 level tbsp mild curry
  powder
1 x 7oz can peeled
  tomatoes
1 carrot, scraped

1 potato, peeled
1 small cauliflower
2 tbsp oil
1 tsp ground cumin
1 tbsp lemon juice
1 bay leaf
½ cup mushrooms,
  chopped

○ Rinse the rice well. Partly cook for about 10 minutes after it has come to the boil. Rinse off excess liquid with cold water. Drain well.

○ Place 2 tbsp oil in a frying pan, and cook the onion over a low heat for 3 minutes. Add half the green and red pepper, cut into small dice, and continue cooking for a further 3 minutes. Tip the rice into the pan with the vegetables. Mix well with seasoning and the garam masala.

○ Oil a ring mold. Mix the remaining oil with the rice mixture and place it in the mold. Bake at 350°F for 15 minutes.

○ Meanwhile, chop half the onion into thin rings.

○ Make a curry paste by chopping the remaining half of the onion and blending it with the garlic, ginger root and curry powder, mixed with 2 tbsp tomato juice.

○ Cut the carrot into rings and dice the potato. Boil in a little salted water for 5 minutes. Drain and retain the vegetable water.

○ Cut the cauliflower into florets, and steep in cold water.

○ Heat the oil and fry the onion rings for 3 minutes. Remove to another saucepan.

○ Fry the curry paste on a fairly high heat until brown. Rinse the pan into the onion saucepan with the remaining juice of the tomatoes and 1¼ cups vegetable water.

○ Add the carrots, the potato, the remaining halves of the red and green peppers, the cauliflower florets, ground cumin, lemon juice, salt, bay leaf, and chopped tomatoes.

○ Bring to the boil and simmer for 25 minutes, stirring well to mix the ingredients and avoid sticking. Add the mushrooms, and allow to simmer for a further 5 minutes. Remove the bay leaf and taste for seasoning.

○ After removing the rice from the oven, leave for a few minutes to shrink. Gently turn the rice ring out of the mold onto a heated serving plate. Pour the vegetable curry into the center of the ring. Turn excess curry onto a separate dish and serve with other suitable curry accompaniments, such as poppadoms and mango chutney.

Calypso Rice

○ ○ ○

This is an everything-but-the-kitchen-sink dish that magically blends a variety of flavors and textures.

SERVES 4

1 scant cup long-grain white rice	1 medium onion, coarsely chopped
1 tsp salt	½ medium red sweet pepper, coarsely chopped
8 ears baby corn	
2oz (½ cup) whole button mushrooms or chopped mushrooms	½ medium green sweet pepper, coarsely chopped
¼ cup water chestnuts, chopped	¼ cup butter or margarine
1 carrot, chopped	1½ tsp soy sauce
1 tbsp coarsely chopped fresh coriander or parsley	¾ cup frozen green peas

○ Preheat the oven to 325°F. Boil the rice in salted water until tender but firm. Drain and set aside in a deep pan. Sauté the baby corn, mushrooms, water chestnuts, carrots, coriander or parsley, onion, and peppers in the butter or margarine until tender. Set aside.

○ Mix the soy sauce into the warm rice. Blend in the vegetables, transfer to a casserole dish, and bake for 15–20 minutes.

○ Cook the peas just before removing the casserole from the oven. Drain the liquid from the peas, mix into the casserole, and serve.

Spicy Okra with Rice

○ ○ ○

SERVES 4

1lb okra
4 tbsp oil
1 large onion, peeled and chopped
1 chili pepper, seeded and chopped
2 tsp cumin seeds
2 tsp coriander seeds
2 cloves garlic, peeled

and crushed
2 tomatoes, peeled and chopped or 1 x 6oz can peeled tomatoes
¼ tsp salt
¼ tsp sugar
2 tbsp lemon juice
⅔ cup water

○ Remove the little end pieces of the okra. Heat 3 tbsp oil in a frying pan and fry until golden for 2 minutes. Remove from the pan.

○ Blend 1 tbsp oil, the onion, chili, cumin, and coriander seeds with the garlic in a food processor or blender. Add a few drops of water if too thick.

○ Heat the oil again in the pan and fry the paste on a fairly high heat for about 2 minutes. Lower the heat. Add the okra, chopped tomatoes, salt, sugar, and lemon juice. Add the water and simmer for 10–15 minutes.

○ Accompany with curry dishes and rice.

Stuffed Zucchini

○ ○ ○

SERVES 4

4 large zucchini
1 onion, peeled
1 red pepper, seeded
1 green pepper, seeded
4 tbsp vegetable oil
1 clove garlic, crushed
¾ cup cooked long-
   grain rice

2 tbsp canned corn
¼ tsp cumin
½ tsp garam masala
salt and freshly ground
   pepper
⅔ cup sour cream
1 tbsp chopped parsley

○ Wash the zucchini and cut a thin slice lengthwise across the top of each. Scoop out the flesh and chop into small pieces. Cut a small slice off the bottom if any of the zucchini are tipping over when laid flat.

○ Prepare the vegetables by dicing the onion and peppers. Heat the oil in a frying pan and cook the onion for 3 minutes. Then add the peppers and garlic. Cook for a further 3 minutes.

○ Add the rice and stir well. Sprinkle in the corn and the seasonings over a low heat, and mix for 1 minute.

○ Brush the zucchini shells with oil, and fill with the rice mixture. Pour the sour cream over the top, and bake at 350°F for 20 minutes.

○ Sprinkle with chopped parsley.

Blue Cheese and Rice Quiche

○ ○ ○

SERVES 4

PASTRY

1 cup flour	2 tbsp shortening
a pinch of salt	1½ tbsp cold water
2 tbsp butter or margarine	

FILLING

⅓–½ cup cooked long-grain rice	salt and freshly ground pepper
¼ lb blue cheese, crumbled	a pinch of cayenne pepper
2 eggs	¼ tsp dry mustard
2 tbsp light cream	2 tsp chopped parsley

○ Preheat the oven to 400°F. Make up the pastry by sieving the flour and salt into a bowl. Add the fat in small lumps and rub in with the fingertips. Add the water, a few drops at a time, and mix to a firm dough. Rest in the refrigerator for 15 minutes.

○ Roll the pastry out in a neat circle to fit a 7-inch pie dish. Lift the pastry over the ring and ease it in. Trim the top. Line with waxed paper and baking beans. Bake in the preheated oven for 15 minutes. Remove the paper and beans, and cook for a further 5 minutes. Allow to cool slightly.

○ Arrange the rice in the bottom of the dish. Mix the crumbled blue cheese with the rice. Beat the eggs. Add the cream and seasonings, then pour over the rice and cheese. Sprinkle with chopped parsley. Bake for 20 minutes at the lower temperature of 350°F.

LEFT **Blue Cheese and Rice Quiche**

Stuffed Baked Cabbage

○ ○ ○

SERVES 4

8 large cabbage leaves

STUFFING

1 tbsp oil	salt and pepper
1 large onion	1 tsp Worcestershire sauce
½ cup long-grain rice	
½ lb mushrooms	

QUICK TOMATO SAUCE

4 scallions, washed and chopped	bouquet garni
	2 drops Tabasco sauce
1 x 15oz can peeled tomatoes	½ tsp sugar
⅔ cup beef broth	½ tsp lemon juice
1 tsp dried basil	2 tsp tomato paste
1 bay leaf	1 tsp cornstarch
	2 tbsp water

○ Place the cabbage leaves in a saucepan with cold water to cover them. Bring them to the boil. Drain. Heat the oil in a frying pan. Add the onion and cook for 3 minutes over a low heat. Put the rice in 1½ cups boiling water with ½ teaspoon salt. Cook for 10 minutes. Rinse and drain.

○ Chop mushrooms and add to onions to brown. Allow to cool. Add seasoning and Worcestershire sauce. Mix, then stir into the undercooked rice.

○ To make up the Quick Tomato Sauce, add the scallions to the tomatoes in a saucepan. Add all ingredients except the cornstarch and water. Bring to the boil and simmer for 20 minutes. After 15 minutes mix the cornstarch and water and add a little hot sauce. Pour the mixture into the sauce and heat until it thickens.

○ Divide the stuffing between the 8 cabbage leaves. Fold and secure with toothpicks. Place in an ovenproof dish, and pour the tomato sauce over the top. Bake at 350°F for 25 minutes. Remove the bouquet garni, bay leaf, and toothpicks before serving.

Eggplant Rice Casserole

○ ○ ○

SERVES 4

2 eggplant, washed
salt
juice of 1 lemon
1 cup long-grain rice
4 tbsp vegetable oil
2 onions, peeled and
   finely chopped
2 cloves garlic, crushed
1 carrot, scraped and
   grated
1 x 15oz can peeled
   tomatoes

1 tsp tomato paste
4 tbsp white wine
4 tbsp broth or water
1 tsp dried basil or 2
   tsp freshly chopped
   basil leaves
¼ lb mushrooms,
   washed and sliced
4 tbsp grated cheese
   (preferably
   Parmesan)

○ Wash and cut the eggplant into thick slices lengthwise. Arrange on a tray lined with absorbent paper towels.

○ Sprinkle with a little salt and lemon juice. Allow to stand for 20–30 minutes.

○ Cook the rice in 4½ cups boiling salted water for 10 minutes. It should still be firm. Drain and toss in

2 tbsp/1oz butter or oil. Place in the bottom of an oiled ovenproof dish or shallow casserole.

○ Meanwhile, heat half the oil in a saucepan and cook the onion and garlic gently for about 4 minutes over a low heat. Add the grated carrot and stir for a further 1 minute.

○ Add the canned tomatoes, tomato paste, white wine, and broth or water with the basil. Stir until the tomatoes are broken down. Simmer gently for 30 minutes.

○ Pat the sliced eggplant dry with paper towels. Heat the remaining oil in a frying pan and fry slices on a medium heat until golden brown. Drain on paper towels.

○ Place slices of eggplant over the rice. Season well. Add half the tomato sauce. Top with a further layer of eggplant and a layer of sliced mushrooms. Pour the remaining tomato sauce over the top.

○ Sprinkle with cheese. Bake at 350°F for 20–30 minutes until the rice is tender.

Stuffed Eggplant

○ ○ ○

SERVES 4

¼ cup brown rice
2 even-sized large
  eggplant
2 tbsp butter
2 tbsp oil
1 large onion, peeled
  and finely chopped

1 clove garlic, crushed
½ lb mushrooms, finely
  chopped
1 x 7oz can peeled
  tomatoes, drained

SAUCE

1½ tbsp butter
3½ tbsp flour
1¼ cups milk

salt and freshly ground
  pepper
2oz (½ cup) mushrooms,
  washed and sliced

TOPPING

¾ cup grated cheese

○ Cook the brown rice in ¼ cup water until tender.

○ Cut the eggplant in half lengthwise. Scoop out the center flesh to make room for the filling. Dice the flesh.

○ Heat the butter and oil in a frying pan, and cook the onions until translucent over a low heat. Add the diced eggplant after a few minutes, and cook for a further 2 minutes. Remove with a slotted spoon onto a plate.

○ Add the garlic to the remaining fat in the pan, and then gradually add the chopped mushrooms and cook until browned. Remove from the heat and mix with the drained tomatoes and other vegetables.

○ Make the sauce by melting the butter in a saucepan, adding the flour, and stirring over a low heat without browning to make a roux. Gradually add the milk, stirring or whisking until smooth. Add the sliced mushrooms.

○ Fill the eggplant with the rice and mushroom mixture, which should be well seasoned. Top with the mushroom sauce and finally with the grated cheese.

○ Place the eggplant in a roasting pan with ½ inch water in the bottom, and then bake at 350°F for approximately 40 minutes.

Rice à la Provençale

o o o

This is a useful recipe to serve with many main dishes as there is no need to cook separate vegetables.

SERVES 5

1 cup long-grain rice	4 zucchini, washed and
2½ cups water	thinly sliced
½ tsp salt	½ tsp basil
4 tbsp oil	4 tbsp white wine
2 tbsp/1oz butter	8 tomatoes, skinned
2 onions, peeled and	and chopped
finely chopped	1 tbsp chopped capers
2 cloves garlic, crushed	2 hard-boiled eggs
salt and freshly ground	8 green olives, pitted
black pepper	2 tbsp chopped parsley
2 red peppers, seeded	or chervil
and blanched	

O Cook the long-grain rice (in 2½ cups water with ½ teaspoon salt) by bringing the water to the boil, adding the rice, and stirring to separate the grains. Cover and simmer gently until the water has all been absorbed, which will take about 15 minutes.

O Heat the oil and butter, and cook the onions over a low heat for about 4 minutes.

O Add the garlic. Dice the blanched peppers, and add with the sliced zucchini, the basil and white wine. Stir gently until cooked for about 5 minutes. Lastly, stir in the tomatoes. Gently fold in the cooked rice and season well.

O Add the chopped capers, and then turn the rice into a heated serving dish.

O Decorate with hard-boiled eggs, green olives, and chopped herbs.

Vegetable Pilaf

o o o

SERVES 4

4 tbsp butter	a pinch of saffron or a
1 medium onion, peeled	few drops of yellow
and thinly sliced	food coloring
1 cup long-grain rice	2 cups broth
salt and freshly ground	
pepper	

O Use an ovenproof casserole for cooking this dish. Heat 3 tbsp butter and cook the onion over a low heat for 4 minutes. Add the rice and stir for another 3 minutes.

O Season well. Add the saffron or coloring to the broth. Then pour the broth onto the rice and mix well with a fork. Bring to the boil. Cover and cook in the oven at 350°F for about 15 minutes, until broth is absorbed and rice grains are separate.

O Add the remaining 1 tbsp butter and, if you wish, 1 tbsp grated cheese.

O Another version of this rice can be made by adding mushrooms, peppers, or grated carrot to the onion.

RIGHT *Rice à la Provençale*

Meaty Main Dishes

Marinated Lamb Chops with Savory Rice

○ ○ ○

SERVES 4

8 best-quality end of neck chops

MARINADE

2 tbsp oil	*salt and freshly ground*
2 tbsp soy sauce	*pepper*
1 tsp brown sugar	*1 tsp lemon juice*

SAUCE

1 onion, peeled	*½ cup canned*
2 tbsp sherry	*pineapple pieces*
2 tbsp water	*1 tbsp parsley, chopped*
2 tbsp redcurrant jelly	*1½ cups Savory Rice*
¼ tbsp ground	*(see Rice Ring,*
coriander	*pages 11 5)*

○ Place the chops in a plastic bag with the mixed marinade. Allow to soak for several hours. Turn the bag around on a dish to help the meat be entirely coated with the marinade.

○ Preheat the oven to 400°F.

○ Arrange the chops on a rack over a roasting pan, and place in the preheated oven. Cook for 15–20 minutes.

○ Make the sauce by adding 1 tbsp oil to a saucepan and cooking the finely chopped onion for 3 minutes. Add the remainder of the marinade from the chops, and simmer for a few minutes. Add the sherry, water, redcurrant jelly, coriander, seasoning, and pineapple pieces. Simmer for 15 minutes. The sauce may be blended before serving. Alternatively, mix 1 tsp cornstarch with 1 tbsp water, add a little warmed sauce, and return to the saucepan. Stir until sauce is slightly thickened.

○ Lay the chops on a bed of Savory Rice, sprinkled with chopped parsley. Pour sauce as you like.

Madras Beef Curry

○ ○ ○

Curries are best made in advance as the spicy flavor improves with reheating. This curry can be cooked on top of the stove, but remember to check from time to time that it is not sticking or drying out. Add a little broth or water if necessary.

SERVES 4

6 tbsp vegetable oil
2 large onions, peeled
4 stalks celery, washed
1½ lb chuck steak
1 tbsp flour
½ tsp paprika
½ tsp garam masala
1–2 tbsp Madras curry
    powder
1 bay leaf

1 tsp tomato paste
2½ cups beef broth or
    water
1 x 15oz can peeled
    tomatoes
1 medium potato,
    peeled
onion rings
1 tbsp chopped parsley

○ Heat 4 tbsp oil in a large frying pan. Cut off a few thin onion rings for garnish, and then finely chop the remainder of the onions and cook for 5 minutes.

○ Remove the strings from the celery and chop finely. Add to the onions, and stir well for a further 2 minutes. Remove to a casserole or thick-bottomed saucepan.

○ Trim the steak and remove any gristle. Cut into 1-inch cubes. Sprinkle with flour seasoned with the paprika and garam masala. Add remaining oil to the frying pan, and fry the meat until golden on all sides. Remove with a slotted spoon to the casserole.

○ Sprinkle the curry powder and any remaining flour into the pan and simmer for 2 minutes. Add the tomato paste to the broth and pour into the pan, stirring well to remove meat juices. Add the canned tomatoes and bring to the boil.

○ Meanwhile, cut the potato into cubes and bring to the boil for 5 minutes in salted water.

○ Add the tomato and curry mixture to the meat and onions. Stir well.

○ Drain the potato cubes, and add to the casserole with ½ tsp salt. Bake at 350°F for 1 hour, or until the meat is tender. Taste and season.

○ Serve with pilau or pilaf rice, mango chutney, and poppadoms, or any of the other side dishes or sambals which are so popular with curry.

LEFT Madras Beef Curry

Souvlakia with Rice

○ ○ ○

*T*his dish is delicious when cooked on a barbecue.

SERVES 4

1lb leg of lamb
12 bay leaves
juice of ½ a lemon
2 tbsp olive oil

salt and freshly ground
*   pepper*
1 tsp oregano
1–1¼ cups long-grain
*   rice, cooked*

○ Allow one skewer for each person. Cut the lamb into 1-inch cubes, and thread onto the skewers with pieces of bay leaf in between. Leave space at either end of the skewers to enable them to rest on the grill rack.

○ Beat the lemon juice into the olive oil, season with salt, pepper, and oregano, and leave the lamb to marinate in the mixture in a plastic bag for at least 1 hour.

○ Broil on barbecue for about 10 minutes, turning occasionally, so that the lamb becomes well seared on the outside and tender and juicy inside.

○ Serve immediately with a tomato and cucumber salad, quarters of lemon to squeeze over the meat, and a dish of cooked rice. Serve lemon juice or seasoned yogurt on all types of accompanying salads.

Red Beans and Rice with Tasso and Andouille

○ ○ ○

*T*he use of two highly spiced meats means this is a spicy dish. You can substitute ham hocks for Tasso, but increase the amount of cayenne and black pepper.

SERVES 6–8

1lb dried kidney beans, picked over	*2 tsp ground cumin*
2–4 tbsp vegetable oil (or bacon fat)	*1 tsp dry mustard*
2 large onions, chopped	*1 tbsp chopped fresh oregano or 1 tsp dried*
4 stalks celery, chopped	*¼ tsp black pepper*
2½ green peppers, chopped	*¼ tsp cayenne pepper*
2 cloves garlic, finely chopped	*6–8 scallions, chopped*
½ lb Tasso, cubed	*1 stalk celery, chopped*
½ lb Andouille sausage, sliced	*½ green pepper, chopped*
2 bay leaves	*3 tbsp chopped fresh parsley*
2 tsp salt	*4–4½ cups cooked rice to serve*

○ In 1 gallon water, soak the beans at least 4 hours. Drain, rinse, and return to the large pot with 6 cups water. Bring to the boil, then simmer, skimming the foam, while you prepare the vegetables.

○ In a frying pan, heat the oil and sauté the onion, 4 chopped stalks celery, the green peppers, and garlic until wilted, about 5 minutes. Add the vegetables to the beans, along with the Tasso, sausage, and seasonings and continue simmering, stirring occasionally, until beans are tender, 1–1½ hours. Add extra water if necessary. Taste and adjust seasonings.

○ Just before serving, stir in the last measure of scallions, celery, green pepper, and parsley. Serve over rice.

Albondiguitas
(Mexican Meatballs) with Salsa

○ ○ ○

The meatballs that make up the famous Albondigas Soup are prepared in a number of other ways. If they are deep-fried, they can be served on their own as a snack or as a meat dish; or with a tomato sauce; or even in a boleta (Mexican roll) to make a torta, the Mexican equivalent of a hoagie or submarine sandwich.

SERVES 6–8

1lb lean ground beef	*2 eggs*
¾ lb ground pork	*chopped coriander*
¾ cup cooked rice	*(optional)*
1 small onion, chopped	*salt and pepper to taste*
very finely	*shortening or oil for*
2 cloves garlic,	*frying*
chopped very finely	

SALSA DI JICAMATE
(BASIC TOMATO SAUCE)

1 x 24oz can tomatoes,	*salt and pepper to taste*
chopped	*olive oil for frying*
6oz can tomato paste	*sugar, if necessary*
2 large onions, finely	*coriander*
chopped	
5–10 cloves garlic	
2–4 serrano chilies	
¾ cup red wine or	
sherry	
pinch each of parsley,	
sage, rosemary,	
thyme, oregano	

○ To make the meatballs, mix all the meatball ingredients together thoroughly. Form the mixture into balls: for a main course, a bit smaller than a golf ball, for appetizers, about 1-inch in diameter. Mexican cooks often insert a piece of hard-boiled egg or half an olive in the middle.

○ Deep-fry for several minutes — it takes a while for the center to be cooked fully. Serve with the Salsa Di Jicamate sauce. You can either fry the meatballs first, or poach them in the sauce.

○ To make the salsa sauce, fry the onions and garlic in 2–3 tbsp of oil. When they are soft and golden, add the serranos, tomatoes, tomato paste, wine, spices, and seasoning. Add sugar if the sauce is too sharp; this will depend on the wine and the tomatoes, and often you won't need sugar. Simmer for 15–30 minutes; add the coriander a minute or two before the end of cooking.

○ You can omit the wine; if you do, omit the tomato paste as well.

Thai Red Pork with Rice

o o o

The red-colored marinade soaks a little way into the meat from the surface; when sliced, the red edges of the pork make this a decorative as well as tasty dish.

SERVES 6

¾lb pork loin
4 cups water
¼ cup tomato paste
3 tbsp white soy sauce
3 tbsp sugar

3 drops of red food coloring (optional)
1½ tbsp cornstarch
2–3 cups cooked rice, heated

NAM CHIM SAUCE

4 tbsp white vinegar
2 tbsp black soy sauce

1 fresh red chili, sliced thinly
¼ tsp sugar

O Mix together the pork, water, tomato paste, soy sauce, sugar, and food coloring in a bowl and leave to marinate for 1 hour. Then put the pork mixture and marinade in a pan, bring to a boil, and simmer for 30 minutes. Remove the pork and roast it in a preheated 350°F oven for 10 minutes. Reserve the cooking liquid.

O Mix a little of the cooking liquid with the cornstarch, and then stir in 2 cups more liquid. Bring to a boil in a small pan to thicken, then remove from the heat.

O Mix together the ingredients for the Nam Chim Sauce. Slice the pork and place on serving plates (on top of the hot rice). Spoon the cornstarch sauce over the top, and serve with the Nam Chim Sauce on the side. Accompany with sliced cucumber, scallions, hard-boiled eggs, and pieces of deep-fried fresh pork fat back or pork belly.

Beef Stroganoff

○   ○   ○

SERVES 4

¾ lb fillet or rump
   steak
2 tbsp butter
2 tbsp vegetable oil
1 small onion, peeled
   and finely chopped
3 scallions, washed
1 tbsp flour
¼ tsp paprika
salt and freshly ground
   pepper

½ lb mushrooms,
   washed and sliced
1 tbsp brandy
2 tbsp madeira or
   sherry
⅓ cup beef broth
5 tbsp sour cream
1 tbsp chopped parsley
¼ tsp paprika
1–1¼ cups long-grain
   rice

○   Trim the steak, and cut into thin strips about 2 inches long. Heat the butter and oil in a frying pan, and cook the onion for about 4 minutes over a low heat until translucent. Add the chopped scallions, retaining a few rings of green stem for final garnish.

○   Meanwhile, mix the flour with the paprika and seasoning, and coat the meat strips evenly.

○   Add the sliced mushrooms to the onions, and sauté gently for another 2 minutes. Remove the onions and mushrooms with a slotted spoon, leaving as much fat behind as possible.

○   Wash the rice well in a sieve or colander under cold water and drain.

○   Add the rice to boiling, salted water and stir through with a fork until the water comes to the boil again. Allow it to boil for about 1 minute. Reduce the heat to allow the rice to simmer very gently for at least 12 minutes. Most of the water should be absorbed after this time; test a grain for tenderness. If the rice is still undercooked, sprinkle 2 tbsp boiling water onto it, and allow to simmer for a further 2 minutes. Keep the rice covered, and leave it to stand for 10 minutes. Fork through gently. The grains should be fluffy and separate.

○   Over a fairly high heat fry the meat for a few minutes, less for fillet steak than for rump. Heat the brandy in a ladle and ignite it with a match.

○   Pour over the steak and allow to flame. Remove the meat and mix with the onion and mushrooms.

○   Add the madeira or sherry and any excess flour and paprika left over to the pan, and stir well. Gradually add the beef broth, scraping all meat juices from the bottom of the pan. Add the meat, mushrooms, and onions to the sauce and reheat for about 2–3 minutes. Turn the heat low. Add 2–3 tbsp sour cream and mix well.

○   Serve in a ring of rice garnished with parsley, sour cream, onion rings, and a sprinkling of paprika. A green salad or crisply cooked green vegetable, such as snow peas or French beans, makes an excellent accompaniment to this luxurious but quickly prepared dish.

LEFT *Beef Stroganoff*

Creole Curried Pork Chops with Rice Pilaf

○ ○ ○

This is a subtly seasoned dish that complements the curried rice. Add a tossed salad for a meal that can be put together in less than half an hour.

SERVES 4

scant 1 cup long-grain
   white rice
2 tbsp vegetable oil
2 cups raisins
½ tsp ground cumin
½ tsp salt
½ tsp freshly ground
   black pepper

1¼ cups chicken broth
¼ cup water
1½ tsp curry powder
⅛ tsp ground cinnamon
⅛ tsp chili powder
8 very thin pork chops
   (2lb in total)

○ Toast the rice in 1 tbsp oil in a saucepan for 2–3 minutes until golden. Stir in the raisins, ¼ tsp cumin, salt, and pepper. Cook for 1 minute. Add the broth and water. Simmer, covered, until the liquids are absorbed by the rice, about 15–20 minutes.

○ Meanwhile, combine the curry powder, remaining cumin, cinnamon, and chili powder. Rub on the chops.

○ Divide the remaining oil between two large frying pans and heat to moderately hot. Divide the chops between the frying pans and cook, covered, for 3 minutes on each side until cooked through. Alternatively, cook in two stages in one frying pan, keeping the first batch of chops warm. Serve with the rice.

Sausage and Bacon Rolls with Tomato Rice

○   ○   ○

SERVES 4

1 cup long-grain rice
2½ cups beef broth
2 tsp tomato paste
1 small onion, peeled
  and chopped

½ tsp salt
8 sausages
8 bacon slices
1¼ cups Spicy Tomato
  Sauce

SPICY TOMATO SAUCE

1 tsp oil
1 onion, peeled and
  finely chopped
1 chili pepper, seeded
  (optional)
1 clove garlic, crushed

1 carrot, scraped and
  grated
1 x 7oz can peeled
  tomatoes
⅔ cup broth or water
1 bay leaf
½ tsp oregano

○ Wash the long-grain rice several times and drain.

○ Mix the beef broth, tomato paste, and onion with the salt and bring to the boil. Pour over the rice, and fork through to stop grains sticking together. Cover and simmer until all liquid is absorbed, about 15 minutes.

○ To make the Spicy Tomato Sauce, heat the oil in a saucepan and cook over a low heat for 4 minutes. Add the garlic and grated carrot. Stir well and then add remaining ingredients. Season well. Simmer for at least 20 minutes on a low heat.

○ Turn the broiler on high and brown the sausages on each side for 3 minutes. Allow to cool slightly, and then wrap bacon slices around the sausages.

○ Broil for a further 5 minutes under a medium heat. Alternatively, cook in the oven in the tomato sauce at 350°F for 15 minutes after browning under the grill.

○ Arrange sausage and bacon rolls on the tomato rice and pour the sauce over the top.

Alma-ata Pilaf

o o o

There are numerous pilaf recipes originating in Central Asia; this one from the capital of Kazakhstan utilizes the rich bounty of fruit which grow there — the apples are particularly famous.

SERVES 6

⅔–¾ cup blanched
   slivered almonds
4 tbsp vegetable oil
1lb lamb steaks, cubed
2 large carrots, cut into
   julienne strips
2 large onions, thinly
   sliced
9–10 dried apricots,
   chopped
6 tbsp raisins

3 cups long-grained
   white rice
salt and freshly ground
   black pepper
1¾ cups chicken broth
⅔ cup orange juice
1 tsp grated orange
   rind
2½ cups water
1 medium red apple,
   cored and chopped

○ Preheat the oven to 400°F. Scatter the almonds on a baking sheet and toast in the oven until golden, about 5 minutes. Set aside and turn the oven down to 350°F.

○ Heat the oil in a large frying pan over medium–high heat. When just smoking, add the lamb cubes and sauté for 6 minutes, or until well browned. Transfer the meat with a slotted spoon to a large casserole.

○ Turn the heat down slightly and sauté the carrots in the oil for 3 minutes, stirring, then add the onions and continue to sauté for another 6 minutes, until the onions are soft and lightly colored. Stir in the dried apricots, raisins, and rice. Cook for 2 minutes, until the rice is coated with the oil and is becoming opaque.

○ Add the rice mixture to the casserole with the meat. Season to taste, then pour the chicken broth, orange juice and rind, and water over the top. Bring to the boil, then cover the casserole and transfer it to the oven. Bake for 40 minutes, or until all the liquid is absorbed.

○ Remove the pilaf from the oven, stir in the chopped apple, and transfer it to a large serving dish, making a neat mound. Scatter the toasted almonds over the top and serve.

Beef Saté

o o o

SERVES 4

2 scallions, washed
1 inch fresh ginger
   root, grated
2 cloves garlic, crushed
8 cardamom pods
1 tsp cumin seeds
1 tsp coriander seeds

juice of 1 lemon
1 tsp grated or ground
   nutmeg
2 bay leaves
2 tbsp oil
1½ lb rump steak

SATÉ SAUCE

6 tbsp peanut butter
1 tbsp brown sugar
2 chili peppers, seeded
1 tsp sugar

juice and rind of
   1 lemon
⅔ cup beef stock
1 cup long-grain rice,
   cooked

○ Place all the ingredients except the meat in a blender to make a paste.

○ Trim the meat and cut into small squares. Mix with the paste and allow to marinate for several hours.

○ Arrange the meat on skewers.

○ Make the sauce by mixing all the ingredients except the lemon juice together in a saucepan. Bring to the boil and simmer for about 20 minutes. Add the lemon juice.

○ While the sauce is cooking, turn the broiler onto a high heat and allow the skewered meat to cook. Turn every 2 minutes for the first 6 minutes, then lower the heat and continue cooking. The time will depend on whether you like your meat slightly rare or well done.

○ Accompany with boiled rice.

Mexican Roast Pork with with Chorizo-Rice Stuffing

o o o

Roast pork is stuffed with a spicy stuffing, then spread with salsa and roasted. Fiery salsas infuse the meat with the heat of the chilies, while milder salsas let the other flavors show through.

SERVES 6

¼ tsp salt
2 tsp olive oil or butter
scant 1 cup white rice
½ lb chorizo sausage
1 small onion, chopped
2 cloves garlic, minced

⅓ cup toasted pine nuts
  (see over)
2 lb pork loin
2 cups salsa

This simple cooked salsa is good with corn chips or as a sauce over eggs or Mexican food. With a few jalapeño seeds included, it is fairly hot. You may use unpeeled tomatoes, but if you wish to remove the skin, dip the tomatoes in boiling water for 30 seconds. The skins should slip off easily.

SALSA
MAKES ABOUT 3½ CUPS

1lb seeded, chopped
  tomatoes
2 cloves finely chopped
  garlic
1 small finely chopped
  onion

4 jalapeño chilies,
  chopped, with some
  seeds included
1 tbsp cider vinegar
1 tsp fresh oregano or
  ¼ tsp dried
salt to taste

○ Preheat the oven to 350°F. Put 2 cups water in a saucepan, add the salt and olive oil or butter, and bring to the boil. Stir in the rice, cover, and reduce the heat. Cook until the water has been absorbed and the rice is tender, 15–20 minutes.

○ To make the Salsa, in a medium saucepan, simmer the tomatoes, garlic, and onion for 10–15 minutes, uncovered, to evaporate excess liquid from the tomatoes. Add the jalapeños, vinegar, and oregano, and simmer for 5 minutes more. Add salt to taste. Set aside.

○ Crumble the chorizo into a small frying pan. Brown over medium heat, 7–10 minutes, then set aside. Discard all but 1 tbsp of fat. Reheat the fat and add the onion. Sauté for 5 minutes, then add the garlic and pine nuts, and cook for 1 minute. Remove from the heat. Mix the chorizo and the onion mixture into the cooked rice.

○ Unroll the pork loin, or make several lengthwise cuts so that it opens as much as possible into a thick, flat piece. Spoon some rice mixture into the center of the loin, then reroll the meat and tie with string. You will have some rice left over. Put it in a lightly greased baking dish, cover, and set aside.

○ Put the pork, cut side up, on a rack in a small roasting pan. Spread some of the Salsa over the pork, but make sure you have some left over for basting. Put the pork in the oven and cook for approximately 1 hour, until the internal temperature measured with a meat thermometer reaches 160°F (although the meat is safe at 140°F). Baste the meat at least once with the additional Salsa. During the last 5 minutes of cooking, put the leftover rice stuffing in the oven.

○ When the pork is done, remove it from the oven and let stand for 15 minutes before carving it into slices. Let the stuffing continue to cook while the pork rests.

○ To toast pine nuts: spread them in a single layer on a baking sheet. Bake at 350°F for 5–10 minutes until they are golden brown. Watch the pine nuts carefully as they burn very quickly.

Liver and Rice Casserole

○ ○ ○

The baking oven came from the east more than a thousand years ago. The old, tried and true Finnish dishes still depend on the oven. In fact, most Finnish cooking makes heavy use of the oven.

SERVES 6–8

1¾ cups white long-grain rice	4 bacon slices, cooked and diced
7½ cups boiling salted water	⅔ cup raisins
3 tbsp butter	2 tbsp corn syrup
1 medium onion, finely chopped	2 tsp salt
2 cups milk	1 tsp white pepper
2 eggs, lightly beaten	1 tsp dried oregano
	1¼lb calf's or ox liver, finely chopped or ground

○ Cook the rice in the boiling salted water for about 12 minutes, then drain and put aside.

○ Melt 2 tbsp butter in a frying pan and gently sauté the onion until golden. Remove and put aside.

○ Preheat the oven to 325°F. In a large bowl, carefully combine the cooked rice, the milk, and beaten eggs. Add the onion, diced bacon, raisins, and corn syrup. Season with salt, pepper, and oregano. Stir in the chopped liver and mix thoroughly.

○ Grease an ovenproof dish and add the liver and rice mixture. Bake, uncovered, for 1–1½ hours. Serve with green salad and loganberry or cranberry sauce.

Coconut Beef Curry

o　o　o

*I*his is one of the driest of Thai curries, and usually quite fiery.

SERVES 8

¼ cup peanut or corn
　oil
¾ lb beef sirloin, cut in
　1¼ x ¾ x ½-inch
　pieces
4 cups thin coconut
　milk
1 tbsp Thai fish sauce

2 tsp sugar
2 fresh red chilies,
　sliced
2 kaffir lime leaves,
　sliced finely
⅓ cup sweet basil
　leaves

CURRY PASTE

6 dried red chilies,
　chopped roughly
7 white peppercorns
18 cloves garlic,
　chopped roughly
3–4 shallots, chopped
　roughly
2 coriander roots,
　chopped roughly

2 tsp salt
1 tsp roughly chopped
　galangal
1 tsp roughly chopped
　lemon grass
1 tsp roughly chopped
　kaffir lime zest
1 tsp shrimp paste

O Pound all the curry paste ingredients together with a mortar and pestle or mix in a blender to form a paste.

O Heat the oil in a pan or wok and fry the curry paste for 3–4 minutes. Add the beef and fry for 2 minutes, then add the coconut milk and boil until the beef is tender, about 15 minutes. Add the fish sauce, sugar, and chili. Remove from the heat, transfer to a serving plate, and sprinkle with the lime zest and basil.

O Serve accompanied by rice.

Sweet and Sour Pork with Rice

o o o

SERVES 4

1lb leg of pork, cut in a
   thick slice
1 small onion, peeled
   and sliced
1-inch fresh ginger
   root, finely chopped
1 clove garlic

1 tbsp dry sherry
2 tbsp soy sauce
salt and freshly ground
   pepper
oil for frying
1½ cups boiled rice

BATTER

3 tbsp cornstarch
2 tsp water

1 egg

SAUCE

1 small red pepper,
   seeded
1 small green pepper,
   seeded
2 scallions, washed
1 cup chicken broth

1 tbsp white wine
   vinegar
2 tsp brown sugar
1 tbsp tomato paste
2 tsp cornstarch

LEFT AND ABOVE *Sweet and Sour Pork with Rice*

O Cut the pork into 1-inch cubes after trimming.

O Mix up the marinade of onion, ginger, garlic, sherry, soy sauce, and seasoning, and allow the pork to stand in this for at least 1 hour, turning from time to time.

O Cut the peppers into ½-inch cubes and chop the scallions into thick rings.

O Place all other ingredients, apart from the cornstarch, into a saucepan with the peppers and scallions. Mix the cornstarch with 2 tbsp of cold water and stir into saucepan. Fry the meat before heating the sauce.

O Make up the batter in a deep plate, mixing the cornstarch, water, and egg together until thick.

O Drop the drained marinated meat into the batter. Make sure the fat is very hot (360°F) before dropping the meat in, either with tongs or a slotted spoon. Cook for about 2–4 minutes until golden. Drain.

O Heat the sweet and sour sauce and, when thickened, add the fried pork. Accompany with plain boiled rice.

Pork Stuffed Cabbage Leaves

○ ○ ○

*K*nown as gotabki in Poland, these may be filled with pork or lamb, rice, a combination of both, or with buckwheat. Gotabki may be made using very large cabbage leaves, serving just one per portion with a little unthickened cooking liquid poured over the top. Alternatively, they may be dressed with a tomato or béchamel-type sauce. Here the cooking juices are thickened and sour cream is added to make a delicious sauce.

SERVES 4

8 large green cabbage leaves	*½ tsp dried oregano*
1 onion, finely chopped	*2 tbsp chopped fresh parsley*
2 tbsp butter	*salt and freshly ground black pepper*
¼ lb (about 1 cup) cooked pork or lamb, diced	*1 cup chicken or beef broth*
½ cup long-grain rice, cooked and cooled	*2 tbsp flour*
¼ lb mushrooms, chopped (use chestnut mushrooms for a good flavor)	*2 tbsp water*
	⅔ cup sour cream

○ Cook the cabbage in boiling water for 2–3 minutes, until pliable. Drain well, dry on paper towels, and trim away a small "V" shape from any hard stalks.

○ Cook the onion in the butter for 10 minutes, until soft. Stir in the meat, rice, mushrooms, herbs, and seasoning. Mix well and cook for 1 minute. Roughly divide this filling into eight.

○ Place a portion of filling on each leaf, slightly nearer the stalk end than in the middle. Fold the stalk end over the filling, then fold the sides of the leaf over. Roll the stuffing and leaf from the stalk end to make a neat parcel. Put into a medium saucepan, join down. Stuff the other leaves and pack them fairly tightly into the pan. If the pan is too large to hold the leaves, use a smaller one. Pour in the broth, and heat until simmering. Cover, and cook for 20 minutes.

○ Transfer the gotabki to a warmed serving dish. Blend the flour with the water and stir into the cooking liquid. Bring to the boil, stirring, then add the sour cream and stir until hot. Taste for seasoning, pour this sauce over the gotabki, and serve.

Crown Roast of Lamb with Apricot Rice Stuffing

○ ○ ○

This is an excellent dinner party dish as it can be prepared in advance.

SERVES 6

2 best ends of neck (lamb)	1 tbsp oil freshly ground pepper

STUFFING

½ cup long-grain or risotto rice	1 tbsp golden raisins
1 tbsp butter	1 tbsp chopped mixed nuts
1 onion, peeled and finely chopped	1 egg, beaten
2 stalks of celery	1 tbsp chopped parsley
12–14 dried apricots, steeped or 1 large can apricots	salt and freshly ground pepper

○ Ask the butcher to prepare the crown roast or, if this is not possible, have the best ends chined. Remove the skin from the fatty side of the joints. Cut along the fat about 1½ inches from the top of the bone, and remove fat and meat from the tops of the bones. Scrape the little end bones clean with a knife. Turn the meat over the cut between the cutlets to enable the joint to bend.

○ Stand the two pieces of meat up with the bones at the top. Turn fatty sides in and sew together at the top and bottom of the joins to make the crown roast. Paint over with oil and sprinkle with pepper.

○ For the stuffing, partially cook the rice for 10 minutes, rinse, and allow to drain and cool.

○ Heat the butter and oil and cook the onion for 4 minutes over a low heat. Add the chopped celery, chopped apricots (if using canned apricots retain 8 drained halves for garnish), raisins, and nuts. Lastly, stir in the rice. Turn into a bowl and allow to cool. Mix with the egg yolk and parsley.

○ Fill the center of the roast with the stuffing. Cover with a piece of foil.

○ Cover the individual tips of the bones with foil to prevent charring. Then completely cover with foil. Roast in the oven at 350°F for 1½–2 hours, depending on size of the cutlets.

○ Any excess stuffing may be used to stuff apricot halves which can be cooked brushed with oil for the last 30 minutes of cooking time.

○ Remove the crown roast to a heated plate, and make gravy to accompany roast in the usual way. If using canned apricots, a little juice may be added to the gravy. Remove the string before carving through the cutlets.

Chili Con Carne

○ ○ ○

SERVES 4

2 onions, peeled
3 stalks celery, washed
2 tbsp vegetable oil
2 cloves garlic, crushed
1lb lean ground beef
1 x 15oz can peeled
  tomatoes
1 carrot, scraped
1–2 tsp chili powder

1 fresh chili pepper,
  seeded
1 green pepper, seeded
1 x 15oz can kidney
  beans
1 bouquet garni (see
  page 36)
1¼ cups beef broth
1 cup long-grain rice

○ Chop the onions finely, and remove strings from the celery before chopping into thin slices.

○ Heat the oil in a frying pan and cook the onions, celery, and garlic over a low heat for 5 minutes.

○ In a thick-bottomed saucepan, heat 1 tbsp oil over a medium heat and brown the ground beef, stirring to keep the meat in small pieces.

○ When the meat is evenly browned, add the cooked onion mixture and the whole can of tomatoes, including the juice.

○ Grate the carrot and add to the meat mixture. Add the chili powder, finely chopped chili pepper and diced green pepper. Finally, add the kidney beans and bouquet garni. Mix well with stock and allow to simmer gently for 40 minutes.

○ Cook the rice by the absorption method (see page 10).

Lamb Tikka with Pilau Rice

○ ○ ○

SERVES 4

1¼ lb leg of lamb (cut
   in a thick slice)

⅔ cup plain yogurt

1 tsp chili powder

1 tsp crushed coriander

1 tsp garam masala

½ tsp salt

juice of 1 fresh lime or
   lemon

1 cup pilau rice,
   cooked

8 lettuce leaves

2 tomatoes, sliced

12 cucumber slices

1 small onion, peeled
   and finely diced

1 lemon or lime,
   quartered

2 rosemary sprigs

○ Leg of lamb sliced about ½ inch thick is best for this dish. Remove any bone or gristle, and then cut into ½-inch thick cubes.

○ Mix yogurt with all other ingredients in a plastic bag or a flat dish. Add the meat to the marinade and allow to soak for several hours. Turn from time to time.

○ Divide the meat onto 4 skewers, and cook in the broiler, turning every 2 minutes.

○ Serve each portion off the skewer with pilau rice, and garnish with a green salad.

73

Red Bean Pork and Rice

○ ○ ○

$\mathcal{F}$rom Central America to the Caribbean to New Orleans, slow-cooked and highly seasoned red beans and rice is a traditional dish. This main-course version uses leftover pork, but it's good with chunks of sausage or shreds of barbecued brisket, too. Top with uncooked salsa for color, crunch, and flavor.

SERVES 6–8

¾ lb dried kidney beans
2–3 tbsp vegetable oil
1 large onion, chopped
2 stalks celery, chopped
3 cloves garlic, put
   through a garlic press
10oz (approximately 2½
   cups) cooked pork
   (diced ham, slivers of
   ham hocks, shredded,
   barbecued, or roast
   pork)

2 bay leaves
1 tsp ground cumin
½ tsp pepper
1–2 tsp salt
5 cups cooked rice
3 cups Salsa Cruda
sour cream

SALSA CRUDA

MAKES ABOUT 2 CUPS

4 medium tomatoes
1 large onion, chopped
5 serrano chilies, partly
    seeded if desired,
    finely chopped
2 cloves garlic, finely
    chopped

3 tbsp chopped fresh
    coriander
2 tbsp lime juice
1 tbsp olive oil
¼–½ tsp salt

○ To make the Red Bean Pork, pick through the beans for pebbles or other debris. Put the beans in a large saucepan, add water, and soak overnight. Or you can bring the beans and water to the boil, boil for 2 minutes, then cover the pan, turn off the heat, and let the beans stand for about an hour.

○ To make the Salsa Cruda, cut the tomatoes in half and squeeze out seeds. Broil the tomatoes cut side down on a flameproof baking sheet until skins are partly blackened

and skins slip off easily. Remove from heat. Let them cool in a colander so excess liquids drain off, and then remove the skins. Purée in a blender or food processor, but do not purée so long that the tomato becomes liquefied.

○ Stir all the remaining ingredients together, and add the tomatoes. Let stand for 30 minutes, then taste and adjust the seasoning.

○ Drain and rinse the beans, and put them back in the pan. Add enough water to cover the beans by about 2 inches, then bring to the boil. Meanwhile, prepare the vegetables. Heat the oil in a frying pan. Add the onion and celery and cook for 5 minutes, then add the garlic and cook for 2 minutes longer. Add the vegetables to the beans, along with the pork, bay leaves, cumin, and pepper. Reduce the heat and simmer until the beans are tender, 1–1½ hours. Check periodically, and add more water if needed. Taste and add salt.

○ Serve the beans over rice, topped with the Salsa Cruda and with sour cream, if desired.

Spanish Pork and Spinach Rice

○ ○ ○

"Sloppy" rice, caldoso, is the Spanish name for this type of dish, which is much easier to make than paella.

SERVES 4–6

¾–1lb lean pork, cubed
6 tbsp olive oil
salt and freshly ground
    black pepper
½ lb fresh spinach,
    washed, trimmed,
    and chopped
8 young garlic cloves
    or whites of fat
    scallions

4 tomatoes, chopped
2 tsp paprika
1½ cups paella or
    risotto rice
pinch of saffron
    strands
7½ cups light broth or
    water, warmed

○ Heat the oil in a paella pan or wide shallow casserole and fry the seasoned pork cubes. When they are golden, spread the chopped spinach over the top and cover with another paella pan, lid, or baking sheet.

○ When the spinach has thoroughly wilted, add the garlic or whites of the scallions and the chopped tomatoes, sprinkling them with the paprika. Cook gently until the tomatoes have reduced. Meanwhile, rinse the rice, drain, and add it with some salt to the pan and stir.

○ Powder the saffron into the warm broth with your fingers, and bring to a gentle simmer. Cook over low heat for 15–18 minutes, until the rice is done. Check the seasoning and stir.

Thai Beef with Spinach

o o o

SERVES 4

1½ lb chuck steak
1¼ cups coconut milk
1 tsp brown sugar
1 tbsp soy sauce
1 tbsp mixed chopped
   nuts
2 cloves garlic, crushed
1 onion, peeled
1-inch fresh ginger root

2 fresh chili peppers,
   seeded
salt and freshly ground
   pepper, seeded
juice of ½ lemon
1 tbsp cornstarch
1lb frozen spinach or
   2lb fresh spinach
4 tbsp yogurt

O Trim off any excess fat from the meat, and cut it into thin strips.

O Put the coconut milk, sugar, nuts, and soy sauce into a saucepan. Mix the beef with these ingredients and bring to the boil. Immediately the mixture bubbles, turn the heat down and allow to simmer for about 10 minutes.

O In a blender or food processor, make a paste with the garlic, onion, fresh ginger, chili peppers, a little salt, and lemon juice. Mix this paste with the cornstarch and a little cold water. Add some of the hot liquid from the beef to the mixture before stirring into the beef. Cover and simmer gently for about 30–40 minutes until meat is cooked and tender.

O Cook the spinach as directed on the package, if using frozen. For fresh spinach, wash and remove large stems and cook in a small amount of boiling salted water for about 5 minutes. Drain cooking water into a bowl, and use to adjust sauce if it has reduced too much. Arrange drained spinach in a hot serving dish.

O Put beef onto the spinach, and trickle yogurt on top.

O Serve with plain boiled rice.

Pineapple Sweet-Sour Pork Balls

o   o   o

SERVES 4

1lb ground pork
1 tsp sesame oil
6 tbsp cornstarch

1 egg
3 tbsp soy sauce
3 tbsp oil

SWEET AND SOUR SAUCE

1 tsp cornstarch
6 tbsp dry sherry
6 tbsp soy sauce
4 tbsp tomato paste
4 tbsp sugar
3 tbsp white wine
    vinegar

1 x 8oz can pineapple
    chunks in syrup
1 large onion, cut in
    chunks
1 large green bell
    pepper, cut in chunks
2 carrots, cut in 1-inch
    strips

O Pound the pork with the sesame oil until well mixed, then mix in the cornstarch, egg, and soy sauce in the same way. Have a plate ready to hold the pork balls. Wash, then wet your hands under cold water. Take small portions of the meat mixture, about the size of walnuts, and knead them into balls. Keep wetting your hands as this prevents the meat from sticking to them, and it gives the balls an even surface.

O Before cooking the pork balls, start preparing the sauce: blend the cornstarch to a paste with 6 tbsp water. Add the sherry and soy sauce, then stir in the tomato paste, sugar, and vinegar. Drain the liquid from the pineapple into the mixture.

O Heat the oil and stir-fry the pork balls until evenly browned and cooked through. Use a slotted spoon to remove them from the pan.

O Add the onion, pepper, and carrots to the hot fat and stir-fry these ingredients for about 5 minutes, until slightly softened. Give the liquid sauce mixture a stir, then pour it into the pan and bring to a boil, stirring all the time. Stir in the pork balls and pineapple and cook, stirring over reduced heat for 3–4 minutes. Serve with plain boiled rice.

Lemon Pork and Rice Balls

○ ○ ○

○ Combine the ground pork, rice, onion, garlic, and herbs in a large mixing bowl. Add the egg yolk and season with salt and freshly ground black pepper. Mix thoroughly to combine all the ingredients. Using slightly damp hands, shape the mixture into 2-inch balls, and then dredge thoroughly with flour.

○ Place the olive oil in a large, deep frying pan with the meatballs. Add enough boiling water to just cover the meatballs. Cover and simmer for 35–40 minutes, or until the meat and rice are cooked, adding a little extra water to keep the meatballs covered during cooking if it appears necessary.

○ To make the lemon sauce, beat together the eggs and lemon juice until frothy. Whisk in 2 tbsp of the cooking liquid from the meatballs, whisking vigorously to prevent curdling. Remove the frying pan from the heat and pour the egg mixture over the meatballs. Return the frying pan to the heat and stir continuously, until thickened. Do not allow the sauce to boil. Transfer the meatballs and sauce to a warm serving dish, and garnish with chopped parsley.

*I*n Greece this dish is called "little spheres." It is a cross between a hearty soup and stew.

SERVES 8–10

1lb ground pork	1 tsp dried oregano
⅔ cup long-grain rice	1 egg yolk
1 large onion, finely chopped	salt and freshly ground black pepper, to taste
2 garlic cloves, crushed	flour, for dredging
4 tbsp very finely chopped fresh parsley	3 tbsp olive oil
	3 eggs, beaten
2 tbsp chopped fresh mint	freshly squeezed juice of 2 lemons, strained
	chopped fresh parsley

Beef Koftas

o o o

SERVES 4

1 medium onion, peeled
  and finely chopped
1 clove garlic, crushed
1lb lean ground beef
1-inch piece fresh
  ginger root, grated
salt and freshly ground
  pepper
½ tsp coriander,
  crushed or ground
1 tsp fresh
  breadcrumbs

1 tbsp yogurt
1 tsp freshly chopped
  parsley
½ tsp lemon juice
1–1¼ cups rice
½ tsp turmeric
2 tbsp oil
2 tbsp chopped
  pineapple
3 tbsp flaked almonds

O Sweat the onion and garlic in a little oil for approximately 4 minutes.

O Mix the ground beef in a bowl along with the ginger, seasoning, coriander, breadcrumbs, yogurt, parsley, and lemon juice.

O Add the onion mixture and mix thoroughly. Form into 8 sausage shapes.

O Meanwhile, put the long-grain rice on to cook with the turmeric and 1 tsp of salt for 15 minutes, when all water should have been absorbed.

O Place the ground beef mixture on wooden skewers. Brush with oil and brown in the broiler, turning every 2 minutes to cook and brown evenly.

O Mix the rice with the pineapple and serve in a heated dish scattered with flaked almonds. Serve the koftas on top. Serve cucumber and pineapple yogurt as a side dish, or a barbecue or curry sauce.

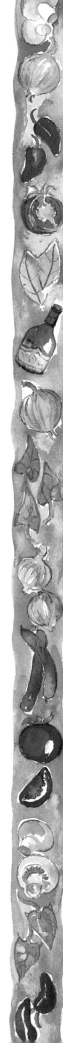

79

Poultry Main Dishes

Braised Chicken in White Wine with Tomato and Rice Stuffing

○ ○ ○

Nutty brown rice is used in the stuffing to make this perfect dinner party recipe. Serve the sauce separately for those who want to control the flow of calories.

SERVES 6

⅔ cup cooked brown rice

3oz garlic sausage, chopped

1 tbsp fresh parsley, chopped

3 tomatoes, skinned, seeded, and chopped

salt and freshly ground black pepper

2 egg yolks

3½ lb oven-ready chicken

1 sweet red pepper

2 tbsp olive oil

1 shallot or small sweet onion, finely chopped

¼ lb large cup mushrooms, thickly sliced

1¼ cups chicken broth

2 tsp cornstarch

3 tbsp light cream

2 tsp freshly chopped basil or ½ tsp dried

○ Prepare the stuffing by mixing together the rice, garlic sausage, parsley, tomatoes, and 1 egg yolk. Season with salt and pepper. Spoon inside the neck end of the chicken and fold the flap of skin over (securing with a small metal skewer, if necessary).

○ Place the sweet red pepper in a hot broiler, and turn until it is blistered all over. Put in a plastic bag and leave to "sweat" for 10 minutes. The skin can then easily be removed. Discard the seeds and thickly slice the flesh.

○ Heat the oil in a large flameproof casserole, add the chicken, and cook over a moderate heat, turning until golden brown all over. Lift out and set aside; add the shallots or onion and mushrooms to the pan, and cook for a few minutes until softened.

○ Return the chicken to the casserole, add the sliced sweet pepper, and pour the wine and broth over the top. Cover and cook in the oven at 350°F for 1 hour 20 minutes, or until tender.

○ Lift the chicken out onto a serving dish, and remove the skewer if necessary. Using a slotted spoon, arrange the mushrooms and peppers around the chicken, and keep warm.

○ Stir the basil into the pan and simmer on the stove for 5 minutes. Beat the remaining egg yolk, cornstarch, and cream together, and stir into the pan. Heat gently until the sauce thickens.

○ Joint or carve the chicken, and accompany each serving with a spoonful of stuffing. Serve the sauce separately.

Gumbo

o o o

Gumbo is a spicy stew of meat and vegetables served over rice. It comes from New Orleans, where cooks include all kinds of meats. This recipe calls for a combination of chicken, shrimp, and spicy smoked sausage.

SERVES 8

4 chicken breasts,
   skinned and cubed
2 tbsp flour
½ tsp salt
¼ tsp black pepper
¼ tsp cayenne pepper
1 tsp paprika
½ tsp onion powder
½ tsp garlic powder
2 tbsp oil
1 large onion, chopped
1 large green pepper,
   chopped
3 stalks celery, chopped
2 cloves garlic, crushed
¼ cup vegetable oil

½ cup flour
9 cups chicken broth
3 medium tomatoes,
   seeded and chopped
¾ lb Andouille sausage
   or other spicy
   smoked sausage,
   sliced
¾ lb medium shrimp,
   peeled and deveined
4–5 scallions, chopped
handful fresh parsley,
   chopped
about 5–6 cups cooked
   rice

○ Mix 2 tbsp flour with the salt and other seasonings. Sprinkle over the cubed chicken and toss so the cubes are evenly coated. Heat 2 tbsp oil in a frying pan and sauté the chicken until it is cooked through and lightly browned, 8–10 minutes. Refrigerate.

○ Have the chopped onion, pepper, celery and garlic ready before you make the roux. Heat the oil in a medium saucepan. The pan should be a little oversized for the quantity you're cooking because the roux gets dangerously hot, and you will want the extra depth in case it splashes around.

○ When the fat is hot, add the flour and whisk it in until the mixture is smooth. Turn the heat to low. Continue cooking, stirring constantly. The roux will turn ivory, then beige, then gradually darken through different shades of brown. Cook until the roux is darker than a golden-brown

bread crust, but has not turned chocolate brown. This will take about 30 minutes over low heat. You must stir constantly to keep the roux from burning. If black flecks appear in the roux, discard it and start again. The burned flavor will permeate the gumbo and ruin it. Never taste or touch the roux, and use extreme caution while stirring; its temperature can reach 500°F.

○ When the roux reaches a medium brown, remove it from the heat. It will continue darkening, even away from the heat source. The way to stop the cooking is to add the chopped vegetables. Gradually and carefully stir in the vegetables until they are coated with roux. Then return the roux to the stove, and cook until vegetables are limp, about 5 minutes. Remove from heat.

○ In a large pan, bring the chicken broth to the boil. Add a few spoonfuls to the roux and stir, then add the roux to the broth. Add the cooked chicken, tomatoes, and sausage. Simmer uncovered for 20 minutes, stirring occasionally. If the sausage is fatty, you may need to skim fat off the top of the gumbo. Taste and adjust seasonings.

○ Just before serving, add the shrimp to the gumbo and cook until they turn white-pink and are tightly curled, 2–3 minutes. Stir in the scallions and parsley, and serve in bowls over rice.

Cajun Duck Rice

○ ○ ○

*U*se leftover duck meat for this delicious, one-dish meal. If you have only a few scraps of duck left, add them to the rice and use it as a side dish instead of a main dish.

SERVES 4–6

2 tbsp duck fat or vegetable oil	*2 tsp fresh thyme or ½ tsp dried*
1 medium onion, chopped	*2 tsp paprika*
½ cup sliced mushrooms	*½ tsp black pepper*
1½ cups uncooked rice	*2 tbsp finely chopped celery leaves*
3 cups duck broth	*8 chopped scallions*
2 tsp salt	*¾ lb (about 3 cups) cooked duck meat, cut into pieces*

○ In a frying pan over medium heat, heat the duck fat or oil. Sauté the onions and mushrooms until the onions are translucent, about 5 minutes. Add the rice and cook until it is lightly browned, about 5 minutes.

○ Meanwhile, in a saucepan, bring the duck broth, seasonings, and celery leaves to the boil. Combine the rice and broth mixtures in a lightly greased 9-cup casserole dish, and stir in the duck and scallions. Cover, and bake at 350°F until all the liquids are absorbed and rice is cooked, about 1 hour.

Yellow Chicken Curry

○ ○ ○

This Indian-influenced curry dish is very popular in Thailand.

SERVES 6

5 cups thin coconut
  milk
1lb chicken, cut into
  medium-sized pieces

1 medium potato,
  peeled and cut into
  1-inch cubes
2 tsp salt
3 tbsp sliced shallots,
  lightly fried

YELLOW CURRY PASTE

5 dried red chilies,
  chopped
10 small garlic cloves,
  chopped
½ stalk of lemon grass,
  sliced
½ tbsp sliced shallot

2 tsp curry powder
1 tsp sliced ginger
1 tsp sliced galangal
1 tsp shrimp paste
1 tsp salt
½ tsp coriander seeds
½ tsp fennel seeds

○ Pound all the curry paste ingredients together with a pestle and mortar or mix in a blender to form a paste.

○ Heat 1 cup of the coconut milk in a wok or pan, and cook the curry paste for 5 minutes. Add the rest of the coconut milk, bring to a boil, add the chicken, and cook until tender, about 10 minutes.

○ Add the potato and salt, and cook until the potato is done, about 10 minutes. Pour into soup bowls and sprinkle with the fried shallots.

○ Serve accompanied by cucumber salad, sliced pickled ginger, and rice.

Caribbean Chicken Pilau

○ ○ ○

SERVES 6

1 onion, chopped
2 garlic cloves
1 tbsp chopped fresh
  chives
1 tbsp chopped fresh
  thyme
2 celery sticks with
  leaves, chopped
4 tbsp water
fresh coconut meat
  from ½ coconut,
  chopped
liquid from fresh
  coconut

1 x 1lb can pigeon
  peas, drained
1 fresh hot pepper
1 tsp salt
freshly ground black
  pepper
2 tbsp vegetable oil
2 tbsp sugar
3½ lb chicken, chopped
1 cup uncooked rice,
  washed and drained
1¼ cups water

○ Grind the onion, garlic, chives, thyme, and celery with 4 tbsp water in a blender or food processor. Empty the mixture into a large saucepan.

○ Make coconut milk using the coconut meat and liquid.

○ Add the coconut milk to the pan, together with the pigeon peas and hot pepper. Cook over a low heat for 15 minutes, then season with the salt and freshly ground black pepper to taste.

○ Heat the oil in a flameproof casserole. Add the sugar and heat until it begins to caramelize.

○ Add the raw chicken to the casserole, and cook for 15 minutes until it has browned. Stir in the pigeon pea mixture, rice and 1¼ cups of water. Bring to the boil, reduce the heat, cover, and simmer for 20 minutes or until the rice and chicken are cooked. Discard the hot pepper before serving.

RIGHT *Caribbean Chicken Pilau*

Turkey Escalopes with White Wine and Mushrooms

o o o

This dish can also be made with veal escalopes.

SERVES 4

2 large turkey breasts,
  boned
1 tbsp flour
¼ tsp paprika
2 tbsp butter
2 tbsp vegetable oil

1 medium-sized onion,
  peeled
¼ lb (about 1 cup)
  mushrooms, washed
  and sliced
2–3 tbsp white wine

SAUCE

1¼ cups milk
1 slice of onion
1 bouquet garni
1 bay leaf
4 slightly crushed
  peppercorns

1½ tbsp butter
3 tbsp flour
salt and pepper
1½ cups savory or plain
  boiled rice

O Cut the turkey breasts in half, and place the halves between a sheet of foil or plastic wrap and beat out to an escalope shape with a rolling pin.

O Mix the flour with the paprika and coat the turkey.

O Heat the butter and oil in a frying pan, and over medium to high heat fry on both sides until golden. They will need about 5 minutes each side. Keep the escalopes warm in a low oven.

O Cut one thick slice from the onion and cut the remainder into fine dice. Over a low heat cook the onion in the pan with oil from the turkey. After 3 minutes add the mushrooms and stir occasionally. Add the white wine and leave for 2 minutes over a very low heat.

O Meanwhile, put the milk with the slice of onion, bouquet garni, bay leaf, and peppercorns on a low heat. Allow to come to almost boiling point. Then turn the heat off. Leave to infuse for 10 minutes, covered.

O Melt the butter in a small saucepan, add the flour and make a roux. Stir for 1 minute, then gradually strain in the infused milk to make a béchamel sauce. Cook until smooth. Add the onion and mushroom mixture, and cook for a further 2–3 minutes.

O Serve with savory or plain boiled rice. Place the escalopes on the rice and pour the mushroom sauce over the escalopes and rice.

Spiced Chicken and Almond Rice

○ ○ ○

SERVES 4

¾ lb chicken breasts
1 tbsp flour
½ tsp paprika
¼ cup butter
scant ½ cup slivered
    almonds
1 onion, peeled and
    finely chopped

2 tbsp vegetable oil
1 cup basmati rice
chicken broth
½ inch fresh ginger
    root, grated
1 tbsp soy sauce

○ Cut the chicken breasts into ⅓-inch strips.

○ Mix the flour and paprika, and thoroughly coat each strip of chicken.

○ Heat the butter over a medium heat, and fry the almonds until golden on each sides. Remove to a plate with a spoon.

○ Lower the heat and cook the onion until translucent for 3–4 minutes. Remove from the pan.

○ Add the oil and, on a fairly high heat, cook the chicken strips for 5 minutes, turning until golden on all sides. Remove from the pan.

○ Wash the basmati rice thoroughly in about 5 changes of water. Drain well before adding to the frying pan. Gradually add the chicken broth, stirring with a fork. Cover, and cook for 15 minutes.

○ Remove the lid and stir in the onions, chicken, and ginger. Gradually add the soy sauce, and cook for about 5 more minutes.

○ Sprinkle the dish with almonds and a little extra paprika. Decorate with a few petals of almonds.

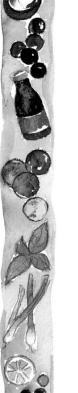

Puerto Rican Chicken and Rice Stew

○ ○ ○

○ Mix the garlic, oregano, and salt together in a large bowl. Add the chicken pieces, and mix them well together. Heat the butter or margarine in a saucepan, and brown the chicken pieces. Transfer them to a plate.

○ Add the onion and green peppers to the pan, and cook until soft.

○ Add the tomatoes and browned chicken pieces, coating them well with the onion, peppers, and tomato mixture. Reduce the heat and simmer for 30 minutes, or until the chicken is cooked.

○ Remove the chicken to a plate and leave to cool a little, until you can handle the chicken.

○ Remove the bones, and then cut the meat into 2-inch pieces.

○ Meanwhile, add the rice, broth, and freshly ground black pepper to the onion, peppers, and tomato mixture, and bring to the boil. Reduce the heat, cover, and simmer for 20 minutes or until the rice is cooked.

○ Stir in the peas, Parmesan, and hot pepper. Mix well, then add the chicken. Cover and simmer for 2 more minutes, then serve.

SERVES 6

1 garlic clove, chopped
½ tsp dried oregano
½ tsp salt
3lb chicken, cut into 8
   pieces
¼ cup butter or
   margarine
1 small onion, finely
   chopped
1 medium green
   pepper, chopped
4 ripe tomatoes,
   skinned and chopped

1½ cups long-grain
   white rice
9 cups chicken broth
freshly ground black
   pepper
1 x 1lb package frozen
   peas
4 tbsp Parmesan
   cheese, freshly grated
1 fresh hot pepper,
   chopped

88

Chicken Saté

o o o

SERVES 4

1½ lb boned chicken

MARINADE

*1 scallion, washed and
  chopped*
*1 inch fresh ginger
  root, grated*
grated rind of 1 lemon
¼ tsp ground cinnamon
6 cardamom pods

1 tsp cumin
1 tsp ground coriander
1 tsp peanut butter
⅔ cup coconut milk

LEFT *Chicken Saté*

SAUCE

6 tbsp peanut butter
*1 onion, peeled and
  finely chopped*
*2 fresh chili peppers,
  seeded*

*1 clove garlic, crushed
  juice of 1 lemon*
*2 tbsp chicken broth or
  coconut milk*

GARNISH

1 scallion, chopped

O Make up the marinade by mixing all the Marinade
ingredients with the coconut milk.

O Cut the chicken into small pieces.

O Marinate the chicken overnight in the refrigerator, or
at least for several hours. Remove from the marinade, and
thread onto wooden or metal skewers.

O Mix all Sauce ingredients together, and cook for 10
minutes. (The best sauce is made by blending all
ingredients together.)

O Broil the chicken on skewers for 4 minutes each side
under a high heat. Then allow to cook for a further 4
minutes each side under a medium heat.

O Serve with boiled rice or a rice salad. Garnish sauce
with chopped scallion.

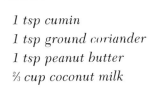

Portuguese Chicken with Rice

○ ○ ○

*T*he Arabs introduced rice-growing to Portugal, and vibrant green paddy fields can still be seen in the lagoons along the west coast. Adding rice is a good way of making meat go further; in this recipe, the *chouriço* adds extra flavor.

SERVES 4

1 large onion, chopped	2½ cups chicken broth
4 tbsp olive oil	½ cup medium-bodied
2 garlic cloves, finely	dry white wine, or
chopped	additional broth
1–2 fresh red chilies,	salt and pepper
seeded and chopped	½ lb chouriço (chorizo),
1 red pepper, cored,	cut into thick slices
seeded, and chopped	1 cup frozen peas
4 boneless chicken	10 oil-cured black
breasts, skinned and	olives, stoned and
cut into thin strips	sliced
1½ cups long-grain rice	2 tbsp chopped parsley

○ Cook the onion in the oil in a large flameproof casserole until softened. Add the garlic, chilies, red pepper, and chicken, and cook gently for 2–3 minutes.

○ Add the rice, broth, wine, and seasoning. Bring to the boil, then cover and simmer for 12 minutes.

○ Stir in the *chouriço* (chorizo), peas, olives, and parsley until just mixed, then cover the casserole and cook for a further 6 minutes, or until the liquid has been absorbed and the rice is tender.

○ Fluff up with a fork, and serve immediately.

Chicken, Andouille, and Shrimp Jambalaya

○ ○ ○

*A*ll the spiciness in this jambalaya comes from the meat. Be sure to taste before you serve, and adjust seasonings, especially if you've had to substitute other ham or sausage for the Tasso and Andouille. This dish is hot and spicy to most people, but not as spicy as traditional Cajun cooking, so add more black and cayenne pepper if you like mouth-searing food.

SERVES 6–8

1 tsp salt
½ tsp cayenne
½ tsp black pepper
1½ tsp fresh or ½ tsp dried thyme
1 whole or 2 half chicken breasts, skinned and cubed
2 tbsp vegetable oil
3 stalks celery, chopped
2 medium onions, chopped
2 medium green peppers, chopped
2 garlic cloves, finely chopped

¼ lb Tasso or other smoked ham, chopped
¼ lb Andouille or other spicy sausage, sliced
1lb tomatoes (about 3–4 medium), seeded and chopped
1 x 8oz can tomato sauce
1 cup poultry or seafood broth
½ lb medium shrimp, shelled and deveined
4 scallions, chopped
3–4 cups cooked rice to serve

○ In a small bowl, mix together the salt, cayenne, black pepper, and thyme. Toss the chicken in the mixture, until it is well coated with spices.

○ In a large frying pan, heat the oil. Sauté the chicken, stirring almost constantly, until the chicken is browned, 6–8 minutes. Add the celery, onion, green pepper, and garlic, and sauté until the vegetables are limp, about 5 minutes.

○ Add the Tasso, Andouille sausage, tomatoes, tomato sauce, and broth, and stir and cook until mixture is bubbling. Reduce the heat, and simmer until tomatoes have cooked down and liquid is slightly reduced, creating a rich, red broth. Add the shrimp and cook until they are opaque and tightly curled, about 2–3 minutes. Taste and adjust the seasonings. It should be very spicy. Add the scallions and enough rice so that the mixture is neither soupy nor dry.

○ Note: if you did not cook the rice with salt, you will need to increase the amount of salt in the jambalaya.

Chicken Biriani

o   o   o

SERVES 4

1 cup long-grain rice, preferably basmati	1 tsp cumin, ground
1 tbsp salt	5 tbsp yogurt
2 large onions, peeled	1 tbsp lemon juice
2 cloves garlic, crushed	4 tbsp water
1-inch piece ginger root, grated	1 tsp ground coriander
6 tbsp vegetable oil	¼ tsp ground cinnamon
2–3 boned chicken portions	½ tsp turmeric
1 tbsp flour	scant ½ cup slivered almonds
¼ tsp chili powder	onion rings
	1 hard-boiled egg
	1 tomato, skinned

O Wash the rice several times. Allow to soak in a large bowl of salted water for at least 1 hour.

O Slice half an onion finely into rings and reserve. Place remaining onion, garlic, ginger, 1 tbsp oil and some water in an electric grinder or food processor with a few slivered almonds. Grind to a paste.

O Heat the remaining oil on a fairly high heat, and fry onion rings until golden brown. Remove with a slotted spoon, and drain on paper towels.

O Fry the remaining slivered almonds until golden on each side, and drain with the onion rings.

O Cut the chicken into small pieces and toss in seasoned flour mixed with the chili powder. Fry until golden and drain on paper towels.

O Fry the paste in fat. Add the yogurt, 1 tbsp at a time, with lemon juice. Add 4 tbsp water, and return the chicken to cook over a low heat for 15 minutes.

O Add the coriander, cumin, and cinnamon to the chicken after 5 minutes, and stir well.

O Meanwhile, cook the rice in 4½ cups boiling salted water with the turmeric for 10 minutes; drain.

O Spread the drained rice on top of the chicken casserole. Add the almonds.

O Cover the mixture with foil and then the casserole lid and bake in the oven for 35 minutes at 300°F.

O Mix the chicken and rice well with a fork, and turn into heated serving dish. Garnish with sliced hard-boiled eggs and browned onion rings. Serve with accompaniments such as cucumber, mango chutney, poppadoms, chapatis, or a vegetable curry.

Oriental Duck

o o o

SERVES 4

1 duck, approximately 4½ lb	4 scallions, washed and chopped

MARINADE

3 tbsp soy sauce	rind and juice of 1 lemon
2 tbsp honey	2 tbsp sherry
½ inch fresh ginger root, grated	2 tbsp vegetable oil

ACCOMPANIMENT

4 tbsp broth or water	1 tbsp sherry and soy sauce (optional)
½ lb water chestnuts	1½ cups boiled rice
½ lb bean shoots	

GRAVY (OPTIONAL)

1 small onion	1 tbsp flour
salt and freshly ground pepper	

O Remove the giblets from the duck. Place the duck in a dish or plastic bag.

O Place half the scallions in a bowl with the ingredients of the marinade. Mix and pour over the duck. Stand in the refrigerator. If you are using a plastic bag, turn the duck from time to time, otherwise, baste the duck. Allow to marinate for several hours or overnight.

O Remove the duck from the marinade. Place it on a rack on top of a roasting pan. Put in the oven at 400°F for 30 minutes to crisp.

O Turn down the heat to 350°F, and cook for a further 1¼ hours.

O Tip the remaining marinade into a saucepan, and bring to the boil. Add the broth or water, and simmer for 5 minutes. Then add the sliced water chestnuts, bean shoots, the remaining scallions, and, if you wish, the sherry and soy sauce. The vegetables should be timed to be served with the cooked duck.

O The duck giblets may be boiled with water, onion, and seasoning to make gravy. To do this, remove the duck from the oven and keep it warm. Pour off the excess fat, leaving the juices behind. Add the flour to the juices. Stir over a high heat, and season well. Add ⅔ cup giblet broth, and whisk until a rich gravy is made. Pour over the carved duck, and accompany with the vegetables and rice.

Nasigoreng

○ ○ ○

This dish originates from Malaysia, and makes good use of any leftover cooked meat, fish, and vegetables. It is quick to prepare, and makes the perfect informal supper dish.

SERVES 4–6

1 cup long-grain rice
4 tbsp groundnut oil
2 onions, finely chopped
1 clove garlic, finely chopped
1 fresh red chili, finely shredded
2 tomatoes, skinned, seeded, and chopped

½ lb (about 2 cups) cooked chicken, diced
6oz cooked shrimp, coarsely chopped
salt and freshly ground black pepper
2 tbsp chopped fresh coriander

OMELET

1 tbsp groundnut oil
3 scallions finely chopped
salt and freshly ground black pepper

2 tbsp light soy sauce
4 eggs, beaten
paprika
cucumber slices

○ Cook the rice until just tender. Drain thoroughly, and spread out on a tray to cool.

○ Heat the oil in a large pan. Sauté the onions and garlic until softened and golden. Add the chili, and cook for a further 2 minutes.

○ Stir in the tomatoes, chicken, and shrimp. Cook for 2 minutes, then add the rice. Stir-fry until the rice turns a light golden color. Season to taste. Stir in the fresh coriander.

○ Mound the rice mixture onto a platter, cover, and keep warm in the oven.

○ For the omelet, heat the oil in a large frying pan. Add the scallions, and cook until softened.

○ Season with salt and pepper, and add the soy sauce. Cook for a further 2 minutes.

○ Stir the beaten eggs into the pan. Cook over a low heat until the omelet is set.

○ Carefully remove the omelet from the pan onto a chopping board. Loosely roll, then shred it finely.

○ Arrange the shreds of omelet over the rice. Sprinkle with a light dusting of paprika, and garnish with cucumber slices. Serve immediately, with extra soy sauce and a selection of salads and relishes.

Chicken Risotto

o o o

A true Italian risotto uses Arborio rice, which contributes to the characteristic creamy texture. If you prefer a slightly "wetter" risotto, add a little more chicken broth (or wine!).

SERVES 4–6

1lb boneless chicken breast, skinned and cubed
2 tbsp sunflower oil
1 onion, finely sliced
2 cloves garlic, crushed
1 tsp dried oregano
1 cup Arborio or long grain rice
1 tbsp tomato paste
5 cups strong chicken broth
splash dry white wine

salt and freshly ground black pepper
6 tomatoes, skinned, seeded, and chopped
10 pitted black olives, halved
1 tbsp chopped parsley or basil
⅔ cup Parmesan cheese, grated

O Heat the oil in a large pan, and cook the onion and garlic over a gentle heat until softened. Add the chicken and cook until golden brown.

O Add the oregano and rice, and cook for a further minute, stirring well. Blend in the tomato paste, broth, and wine. Season to taste, and stir well.

O Cook over a gentle heat for 25 to 30 minutes, or until all the liquid has been absorbed, but the rice still has a nutty bite to it.

O Lightly fork in the tomatoes, olives, and chopped parsley or basil. Heat through for a further 2 minutes. Serve, sprinkled with the Parmesan cheese.

Bokari Pilaf

o o o

SERVES 4

1lb chicken livers
4 tbsp vegetable oil
2 onions, peeled and diced
1 clove garlic, crushed
2 carrots, scraped and grated
1½ cups basmati or long-grain rice

salt and freshly ground pepper
½ tsp turmeric
2½ cups chicken broth
1 x 7oz can tomatoes or 3 tomatoes, skinned
2 tbsp parsley, chopped

O Trim and dice chicken livers.

O Heat the oil in a large pan, and fry the livers until golden brown.

O Add the onions, garlic, and carrots to the chicken livers, and turn with a spoon for about 2 minutes.

O Add the washed rice, seasoning, turmeric, and broth. Cover and cook for 20 minutes. Remove the lid and stir gently. Add the chopped tomatoes, and cook for a further 5–10 minutes until the rice is tender.

O Turn into a heated serving dish and sprinkle with chopped parsley.

LEFT *Chicken Risotto*   TOP RIGHT *Bokari Pilaf*

Spanish Rice with Chicken Livers

○ ○ ○

SERVES 4

1 cup long-grain rice
2½ cups chicken stock
* or water*
1 tsp salt
½ tsp turmeric
2 tbsp vegetable oil
¼ lb chicken livers,
* trimmed and*
* chopped*
1 onion, peeled and
* finely chopped*

6 tomatoes, peeled and
* chopped or 1 x 15oz*
* can peeled tomatoes*
salt and freshly ground
* pepper*
¼ tsp sugar
2 red peppers, seeded,
* chopped, and*
* blanched*
1 cup thawed petits
* pois*
¼ lb cooked shrimp

○ Cook the long-grain rice with boiling water or broth to which the salt and turmeric has been added. Cook by absorption method (see page 10).

○ Meanwhile, heat the oil in a frying pan, and over a medium heat fry the chopped chicken livers until golden brown. Turn the heat down and add the onion. Cook, stirring well, for 4 minutes. Add the tomatoes, salt, pepper, sugar, and chopped peppers. Stir gently.

○ Add the thawed peas and shrimp. Heat through in the vegetable mixture, and mix in the warmed rice.

○ Turn out into a dish and serve hot. A little butter may be added, if you like.

Coriander Chicken with Pilau Rice

○ ○ ○

𝒯resh coriander has a unique, pungent flavor.

SERVES 4

1 tbsp sunflower oil
8 chicken thighs
1 large onion, sliced
1 tsp paprika
1 tsp ground cumin
½ tsp dried thyme
freshly ground black
 pepper

1¼ cup well-flavored
 chicken broth
¼ cup pitted black
 olives
2 tbsp fresh coriander,
 finely chopped
squeeze lemon juice

PILAU RICE

2 tbsp vegetable oil
½ cup whole blanched
 almonds, toasted
1 small onion, finely
 diced

⅓ cup raisins, either
 brown or golden
1½ cups long-grain rice
3 cups boiling water
½ tsp salt

○ Heat the oil in a large pan, and fry the chicken until an even, rich brown. Transfer to a plate.

○ Add the onion to the remaining oil, and cook until softened and golden. Stir in the paprika, cumin, and turmeric, and cook for a further minute. Add the thyme, black pepper, and broth, and bring to the boil.

○ Return the chicken to the pan, skin side down. Cover and simmer for 1 to 1¼ hours, or until the chicken is cooked and tender.

○ Remove the chicken with a slotted spoon to a heated serving dish, and keep warm.

○ Reduce the sauce by rapidly boiling until it thickens. Stir in the olives, coriander, and lemon juice. Season to taste, and pour over the chicken.

○ For the rice, heat the oil in a large pan and cook the onion until softened but not colored. Add the toasted almonds, raisins, and rice, and cook for a further minute, stirring thoroughly.

○ Add the boiling water and salt. Bring to the boil, then cover and reduce the heat to a simmer. Cook for 15 minutes, or until all the water has been absorbed and the rice is tender, but still firm. Fork the rice lightly and serve with the chicken.

Seafood Main Dishes

Shrimp Fried Rice

Paella Valenciana

Shrimp Creole

Salmon Coulibiac

Cajun Seafood Gumbo with Okra

Tuna and Rice Stuffed Peppers

Broiled Jumbo Shrimp
with Rice and Tomato Sauce

Curried Halibut Fillets

Caribbean Shrimp and Tomato Rice

Crab Pilau

Seafood Jambalaya

Kedgeree

Scandinavian Curried Cod

Salmon with Dill and Ginger
Vinaigrette

Shrimp Fried Rice

○ ○ ○

SERVES 4–6

2 tbsp vegetable oil
1lb shrimp, peeled
1 scallion, chopped
½ cup fresh button
    mushrooms
1 zucchini, thinly sliced
½ carrot, thinly sliced
2oz French beans, cut
    into 1-inch lengths

1 tbsp rice wine or dry
    sherry
1 tsp light soy sauce
freshly ground black
    pepper
salt
3–3½ cups plain boiled
    rice
2 scallions, neatly
    chopped into rounds

○ Heat ½ tbsp oil in a wok, and stir-fry the shrimp for 1 minute. Remove and set aside.

○ Add the remaining oil and sweat the scallion. Add the mushrooms and the other vegetables, and stir-fry for 2 minutes over a high heat.

○ Put the shrimp back into the wok with the vegetables, and add the rest of the ingredients except the rice, continuing to stir all the while.

○ Add the rice and stir-fry until the rice has changed color. Place in a large serving bowl, and garnish with the chopped scallions.

Paella Valenciana

○ ○ ○

*T*his great star turn of the Valencian coast has always been cooked outdoors. Preparing it takes all morning, and it is cooked by the men, so the whole thing becomes a party. The ingredients for it are rather special. It originally included snails, and still has three sorts of beans in Valencia. This is a more modest version, but it still needs good broth and a suitably shallow, wide 13–14-inch paella pan.

It speeds things up to prepare the base for the rice in the paella pan, and to use a second pan for frying the shellfish and chicken pieces.

SERVES 6

1½ cups paella or risotto rice
4–5 tbsp olive oil
1 onion, chopped
2 garlic cloves, finely chopped
5 cups fish broth
1 cup dry white wine
15 saffron strands soaked in 2 tbsp hot water, or saffron powder
½ lb raw shrimp, peeled
salt and freshly ground black pepper

pinch of cayenne pepper
6 chicken thighs or 3 legs, halved
½ lb mussels, cleaned
1 tsp paprika
¼ lb (about 1 cup) cooked green beans or peas
1 x 7oz can red pimentos, drained
3 tbsp chopped fresh parsley

○ Fry the onion in 2 tbsp of oil in the paella pan (the rice pan), adding the garlic when it softens. Warm the broth and wine together, soaking the saffron in a cupful of it.

○ Meanwhile, start a second frying pan, heating 2 tbsp of oil. Fry the peeled shrimp for 2 minutes (skip this if they are already boiled), then reserve.

○ Rub salt, pepper, and the cayenne pepper into the chicken pieces, and fry for about 10 minutes on each side, adding more oil if needed.

○ Wash the rice in a sieve and drain. Add the rice to the onion in the paella pan, stir for a couple of minutes' and sprinkle with the paprika. Add the saffron liquid and ⅓ of the broth and bring back to the boil. Set the kitchen timer for 20–25 minutes. When the liquid has been absorbed, add another third of the broth and distribute the mussels, shrimp, and beans or peas round the pan.

○ When the liquid has nearly gone, add the remaining broth and give the mixture its last stir. Add the chicken pieces, bedding them into the liquid around the pan. Simmer on the lowest heat (best on a heat diffuser) for about 8–10 minutes. The liquid should all disappear by the time the timer rings. Check that the rice is cooked.

○ Cut the pimentos into strips and lay these across the rice. Then turn off the heat and wrap the paella pan in newspaper or foil to keep in the steam. Let it stand for 10 minutes. The flavors will blend, and the last drop of liquid should disappear. Sprinkle with parsley, and serve. Spaniards drink red wine with paella.

Shrimp Creole

○ Heat the oil in a large saucepan, frying pan, or wok. Add the onion, garlic, celery, tomatoes, and peppers, and fry over moderate heat until tender. Then add the tomato paste, hot pepper sauce, oregano, and thyme, and blend, stirring constantly, for about 2 minutes.

○ Add the Worcestershire sauce and chicken broth, and bring to the boil over medium-high heat until thickened, about 30 minutes.

○ Add the shrimp and water chestnuts and simmer, uncovered, until the shrimp are opaque throughout, about 4 minutes.

○ Remove from the heat, and adjust the seasoning with more hot pepper sauce to taste, the lime juice, salt, and pepper.

○ Serve over a scoop of rice on warm dishes, and sprinkle coriander or parsley over the top. Serve immediately.

RIGHT *Salmon Coulibiac*

The liquid in this version of Shrimp Creole is reduced until the sauce becomes very thick and flavorful. The water chestnuts add a crunchy Oriental texture.

SERVES 4–6

2 tbsp vegetable oil
1 large onion, chopped
8 cloves garlic, finely chopped
2 large celery sticks, finely chopped
4 medium tomatoes, chopped
2 medium green sweet peppers, chopped
2 tbsp tomato paste
1 tsp hot pepper or Tabasco sauce
½ tsp dried oregano
1 tsp dried thyme

2 tsp Worcestershire sauce
5½ cups chicken broth
1½ lb shrimp, shelled and deveined
1 x 8oz can sliced water chestnuts, drained and rinsed
½ tbsp lime juice
salt and freshly ground black pepper
4–5 cups cooked white long-grain rice
1 tbsp chopped coriander or parsley

Salmon Coulibiac

○ ○ ○

SERVES 4

1lb fresh salmon
2 tbsp white wine
1 bay leaf
1 bouquet garni

⅔ cup water
freshly ground pepper
½ onion

FILLING

¼ cup butter
1 onion, peeled and
  finely chopped
¼ lb mushrooms,
  washed and sliced
1¼ cups cooked long-
  grain rice

1 tbsp chopped parsley
¼ tsp chopped dill
salt and freshly ground
  pepper
2 hard-boiled eggs,
  shelled and chopped

PASTRY

1lb frozen puff pastry,
  thawed

1 egg

○ Place the salmon in a deep saucepan, preferably on a trivet. If this is not available, place the fish on a piece of double foil, with two ends reaching up the sides of the saucepan, as this will make it easy to remove.

○ Place the white wine, bay leaf, bouquet garni, water, pepper, and onion in a saucepan, and bring to the boil; simmer for 10 minutes.

○ Pour the liquid over the salmon, and bring to the boil again. Turn the heat low as the salmon must be allowed to poach very gently for 15 minutes. Allow less time if the fish is in steaks. The liquid should only move slightly in the saucepan. Allow to cool in the fish liquor.

○ Remove the fish from the saucepan, and take off the skin. Remove any bones, and flake.

○ For the filling, heat the butter in a frying pan and cook the onion over a low heat for 4 minutes. Push to one side of the pan.

○ Add the mushrooms. Cook for 3 minutes. Add the rice, herbs, and seasoning. Mix, and allow to cool.

○ Divide the pastry into 4 pieces. Roll out one piece of pastry on a work surface into an 8-inch square.

○ Divide the rice mixture into 4 portions and the salmon into 4 equal servings. Put half the first rice portion in the center of the rolled-out pastry, and place 1 salmon portion on top. Finally, cover the other half of the first rice portion. Damp the edges of the pastry with cold water, and fold the corners to the center. Pinch the edges together, enclosing the filling. Repeat for the other 3 pastry parcels.

○ Flake and flute the edges of the pastry, and decorate with pastry leaves. Rest in the refrigerator for 20 minutes. Glaze with beaten egg, and cook in a preheated oven at 425°F for 30 minutes, until golden brown.

○ Serve accompanied with hollandaise sauce.

Cajun Seafood Gumbo with Okra

○ ○ ○

Okra is used as the thickener, so this mildly spicy gumbo is lighter than a roux-based gumbo. Use at least three different types of fish and shellfish.

SERVES 8

2 tbsp vegetable oil
2 large onions, chopped
2 large green peppers, chopped
2 stalks celery, chopped
3 garlic cloves, finely chopped
3 large or 4 medium tomatoes, seeded and chopped
1 x 8oz jar tomato sauce
7½ cups seafood stock
1 tbsp fresh-squeezed lemon juice
2 bay leaves

1 tbsp fresh thyme or 1 tsp dried
1 tsp salt
¼ tsp black pepper
large pinch cayenne
large pinch white pepper
½ tsp paprika
1½ lb okra, thawed and well drained if frozen, sliced
2lb mixed seafood
3–4 cups cooked rice to serve
filé powder (optional)

○ In a large frying pan, heat the oil. Sauté the onion, pepper, celery, and garlic until limp, about 5 minutes. Transfer to a large saucepan or stockpot and add the tomatoes, tomato sauce, seafood stock, lemon juice, and seasonings. Bring to the boil, then reduce the heat and simmer, uncovered, 5 minutes.

○ Add the okra and return to the boil, then reduce the heat and simmer 30 minutes. Add the seafood: cubed fish and frogs' legs take the longest times to cook, oysters the least.

○ Spoon the rice into individual large bowls. Ladle the gumbo over the rice. If desired, add a pinch of filé powder to each bowl.

Tuna and Rice Stuffed Peppers

○ ○ ○

SERVES 4

4 red or green peppers
¼ cup long-grain rice
a pinch of saffron
   powder or turmeric
2 tbsp butter
1 onion, chopped
1 clove garlic, crushed
¼ lb mushrooms, thinly
   sliced and blanched

1 x 6oz can tuna fish,
   drained, or ¼ lb
   peeled shrimp,
   chopped
1 tbsp chopped parsley
salt and freshly ground
   pepper
1¼ cups Spicy Tomato
   Sauce (see page 63)

○ Blanch the whole peppers in salted water. Drain. Cut off the tops and scoop out the seeds.

○ Cook the rice with a pinch of saffron or turmeric in boiling salted water for 15 minutes until just cooked.

○ Strain, and rinse in cold water. Drain well.

○ Melt the butter and soften the onion and garlic. Add the mushrooms, tuna, rice, and parsley. Mix well, and season to taste.

○ Spoon stuffing into the peppers, and place in a well-greased dish. Cover with buttered paper or foil. Surround with the tomato sauce, and bake in a moderate oven at 350°F for 30 minutes.

○ Sprinkle with any extra parsley.

Broiled Jumbo Shrimp with Rice and Tomato Sauce

o o o

This is a Portuguese recipe. The fishing port of Peniche, on the coast of Portugal above Lisbon, is famed for its shellfish, particularly spiny lobster and jumbo-sized shrimp.

SERVES 4

1 onion, finely chopped	olive oil for basting
1½ cups long-grain rice	salt and pepper
3 tbsp butter	about 2–3 tbsp
1½ lb raw jumbo	chopped parsley
shrimp in their shells	

SAUCE

1 onion, chopped	1 bouquet garni
1 garlic clove, chopped	⅔ cup medium-bodied
1½ tbsp oil	dry white wine
1¼ lb well-flavored	12 oil-cured pitted
tomatoes, seeded and	black olives
chopped	

O To make the sauce, cook the onion and garlic in the oil until softened but not colored. Stir in the tomatoes and cook for a few minutes before adding the bouquet garni, wine, and olives. Simmer gently until it has thickened.

O Meanwhile, cook the onion and rice in the butter, stirring, until golden. Add water to cover generously, and bring to the boil. Cover the pan and simmer for about 12 minutes until tender.

O Preheat the broiler. Thread the shrimp on skewers, brush with oil, and broil for 7–8 minutes, turning occasionally.

O Drain the rice, rinse quickly with boiling water, and stir in the parsley and seasoning.

O Season the sauce and discard the bouquet garni. Serve the shrimp on a bed of rice, accompanied by the sauce.

Curried Halibut Fillets

o o o

𝒯his dish comes from one of the Jewish communities in India, the southern city of Cochin. Cochin is near the Kerala Coast, which produces fresh fish and is also famous for its spice market.

SERVES 6

1 tbsp vegetable oil
1 onion, cut in half and
   thinly sliced
2–3 garlic cloves,
   peeled and finely
   chopped
2lb halibut fillets, cut
   in 3-inch pieces
3 tbsp fresh coriander
   leaves, chopped

1 tbsp red wine vinegar
4 tbsp tomato paste
1 tsp ground cumin
½ tsp turmeric
1 small fresh red chili,
   or ½ tsp red-pepper
   flakes
hot boiled rice for
   serving

○ In a large frying pan, over medium–high heat, heat oil. Add sliced onions, and cook until softened and beginning to color, 3–5 minutes. Add garlic and cook another minute longer.

○ Add fish, and cook until the fish begins to firm and turn opaque, 4–5 minutes. Gently stir in remaining ingredients, except rice, and ½ cup water and simmer 15 minutes, covered. The fish will flake easily if tested with the tip of the knife.

○ Remove fish fillets to a serving dish. Increase heat to high, and cook sauce until slightly thickened, 2–3 minutes. Pour over fish fillets. Garnish with coriander sprigs and serve with hot rice.

Caribbean Shrimp and Tomato Rice

○ ○ ○

SERVES 4

2 tbsp olive oil

1 garlic clove, crushed

2 tomatoes, peeled and chopped

1 tsp saffron

2 tsp salt

1 tsp paprika

3 cups peas

1½ cups uncooked rice

freshly ground black pepper

2½ cups water

8 small shrimp, cooked, shelled, and deveined

12 jumbo shrimp, cooked, shelled, and deveined

○ Heat the oil in a saucepan, then fry the garlic in it for 2 minutes.

○ Add the tomatoes, saffron, salt, paprika, peas, rice, and freshly ground black pepper, fry for 5 minutes, then add the water to the pan.

○ Add the shrimp and cook for 15 more minutes, or until the rice has cooked (if necessary, adding some more water). Serve immediately.

○ Serve with a cucumber salad.

Crab Pilau

○ ○ ○

This recipe for rice with crab and coconut milk originated in Tobago.

SERVES 6

2 tbsp butter or
  margarine
2 tbsp vegetable oil
1 medium onion,
  chopped
1 garlic clove, chopped
½ tsp hot pepper,
  chopped
5 tsp curry powder
2 cups uncooked long-
  grain white rice,
  washed

5½ cups coconut milk
1 tsp salt
freshly ground black
  pepper
1lb fresh, canned, or
  frozen crabmeat
1 tbsp fresh lime
2 tbsp raisins

○ Melt the butter or margarine in a large saucepan over a medium heat. Add the oil, onion, garlic, and hot pepper, and cook for 5 more minutes.

○ Add the curry powder and stir in, then add the rice and cook for 3 minutes.

○ Add the coconut milk, salt, and freshly ground black pepper to taste, and bring to the boil over a high heat. Reduce the heat, cover, and simmer for 15 minutes.

○ Add the crabmeat and lime or lemon juice, and simmer for 5 more minutes or until the liquid has been absorbed. Decorate with the raisins and serve hot.

○ Serve with a cucumber salad.

Seafood Jambalaya

○ ○ ○

Jambalaya is traditionally made with ham, but it's not a necessity. You may add ham, if you desire — ¼–½ lb chopped ham — and if you use Tasso ham, you may need to decrease the seasonings.

SERVES 6–8

2 tbsp vegetable oil
1 onion, chopped
1 green pepper,
  chopped
2 stalks celery, chopped
3 cloves garlic, finely
  chopped
3 large tomatoes,
  seeded and chopped
1 x 8oz can tomato
  sauce
1 cup seafood broth
3–4 tbsp chopped fresh
  parsley
2 bay leaves

1 tbsp fresh thyme or 1
  tsp dried
1 tsp salt
¼ tsp black pepper
½ tsp cayenne
large pinch white
  pepper
2lb fresh shrimp, crab
  meat, crawfish, or
  oysters, or any
  combination,
  prepared
4–6 scallions, chopped
3–4 cups cooked rice to
  serve

○ Heat the oil in a deep frying pan. Sauté the onion, green pepper, celery, and garlic for about 5 minutes. Add the tomatoes, tomato sauce, broth, parsley, and seasonings, then simmer until the tomatoes are cooked down and the liquids reduced. Taste and adjust seasonings.

○ Add the seafood. (If using oysters, cut into bite-sized pieces and add in last 2–3 minutes of cooking.) Simmer just until the shrimp are opaque and tightly curled, 5–7 minutes. Just before serving, mix in the scallions. Serve over rice.

RIGHT *Seafood Jambalaya*

Kedgeree

∘ ∘ ∘

*T*his makes an excellent breakfast dish for guests as it can be prepared in advance and heated through just before serving.

SERVES 4

½ cup long-grain rice
3 hard-boiled eggs,
  shelled
salt and freshly ground
  pepper
½ lb smoked haddock

⅔ cup milk
1 bay leaf
1 slice of peeled onion
1 tbsp chopped parsley
½ tsp paprika
1 lemon, quartered

O Cook the rice by the absorption method (see page 10).

O Chop 2 hard-boiled eggs. Sieve the white and yolk of the third egg separately to garnish the kedgeree.

O Add the chopped eggs to the rice, with salt and pepper.

O Place the smoked haddock in a saucepan with the milk, bay leaf, onion, and a little pepper. Bring to the boil, and allow to simmer for 5 minutes. Allow to cool slightly in the milk. Remove, and flake the fish from the skin. Add to the rice.

O Heat all the ingredients together and pile onto a heated serving dish.

O Garnish with rows of egg yolk, egg white, and chopped parsley with a little paprika. Serve with lemon quarters.

Scandinavian Curried Cod

∘ ∘ ∘

*T*his curry sauce is equally good with chicken. Fried almonds add a delicious touch. Lettuce dressed with lemon vinaigrette is a good accompaniment.

SERVES 4–6

1¼ cups water
1 cup dry white wine
1 small leek or onion,
  sliced
5 white peppercorns

1½ tsp salt
1–1¼ lb cod fillets
boiled long-grain rice
almonds or salted
  peanuts fried in oil

CURRY SAUCE

2 tbsp butter
1½ tsp curry powder
2 tbsp flour
1⅓ cups strained fish
  broth

1 egg yolk
½–1 cup cream
salt and pepper

O Mix the water, wine, leek or onion, peppercorns, and salt in a pan. Bring to the boil, cover, and simmer for 10 minutes.

O Rinse the fish fillets, fold them double, and place in a wide saucepan. Strain the liquid and pour onto the fish. Simmer for 6–8 minutes.

O For the sauce, melt the butter, add the curry powder and flour, and heat without browning. Add the fish broth gradually, stirring, and simmer for a few minutes. Remove from the heat and whisk in the egg yolk with the cream. Season.

O Place the fish on a bed of boiled rice and pour some of the sauce on top. Serve the rest separately. Garnish with fried almonds or salted peanuts.

Salmon with Dill and Ginger Vinaigrette

o   o   o

This recipe uses a cold water fish but gives it a Caribbean spice treatment. Serve with a Creole rice-and-beans dish (see page 24).

SERVES 4

4 x 6oz boneless salmon fillets with skin on	salt
9 large sprigs fresh dill	9 whole black peppercorns
1 bay leaf	2 tbsp white wine vinegar
4 whole cloves	

DILL AND GINGER VINAIGRETTE

2 tbsp French mustard	2 tbsp tarragon vinegar
1 tbsp grated ginger root	2 tbsp canned pimentoes, diced
2 tbsp finely chopped shallot	salt and freshly ground black pepper
1 tsp finely chopped garlic	½ cup olive oil

○ Prepare the vinaigrette by whisking the mustard, ginger, shallot, garlic, vinegar, pimentoes, and salt and pepper together in a bowl. Then add the olive oil in a slow stream, whisking rapidly until well blended. Set aside.

○ Place the salmon fillets in a shallow saucepan with enough water to cover. Add all but one dill sprig, the bay leaf, cloves, salt, peppercorns, and vinegar. Bring the water to the boil, and simmer for 3–5 minutes. Do not overcook. Drain and serve with the vinaigrette, giving the vinaigrette a last-second whisking, if necessary. Float the reserved sprig of dill on top of the bowl of vinaigrette.

Desserts

Rice Meringue

○ ○ ○

SERVES 4

¼ cup short-grain rice
½ tbsp butter
2½ cups milk
rind of 1 lemon

3 tbsp sugar
2 eggs, separated
2 tbsp raspberry jam
½ cup sugar

○ Wash the rice several times in a sieve under the cold faucet. Drain.

○ Butter an ovenproof dish, and sprinkle the rice into the dish. Cover with the milk, lemon rind, and 3 tbsp sugar. Stir well.

○ Cook in the oven at 300°F for 30 minutes. Remove, add the egg yolks, and stir well. Cover with foil, and continue cooking for a further 1 hour.

○ Remove from the oven and spread the surface with jam. Allow to cool slightly.

○ Whisk the egg whites until light and fluffy. Add half the sugar and continue whisking until the mixture is glossy. Fold in the remaining sugar, keeping back ½ tsp to sprinkle on top.

○ Pile the meringue mixture on top of the pudding and sprinkle with sugar. Return it to the oven at the higher temperature of 350°F, and bake for 25 minutes, when the topping will be golden and crisp on top.

Cajun Rice Pudding

○ ○ ○

Rice pudding is a great way to use leftover rice. You may find yourself intentionally making too much rice for dinner, just so you have an excuse to make this old-fashioned custard dessert.

SERVES 6

3 tbsp milk
½ tbsp butter, melted
4 eggs, lightly beaten
⅓ cup sugar
1 tsp vanilla essence

1 tsp grated lemon peel
½ tsp cinnamon
¼ tsp grated nutmeg
½ cup raisins
1½ cups cooked rice

○ In a large bowl, mix all the ingredients together, except the rice: spices have a tendency to clump, so use a wire whisk. Stir in the rice.

○ Pour into a buttered casserole dish and bake at 325°F until the custard sets, about 1 hour, stirring once after about 15 minutes. Serve warm.

Calas

o o o

These sweet rice cakes are deep-fried, sprinkled with powdered sugar, and served for breakfast like small pastries. They are delicious hot, and it's hard to stop with just one or two.

MAKES ABOUT 20

2 eggs
5 tbsp sugar
2 tsp vanilla essence
½ tsp grated nutmeg
½ tsp grated lemon peel
½ tsp salt

2 tsp baking powder
1¼–1½ cups cold
  cooked rice
1 cup flour
vegetable oil for frying
powdered sugar

O In a mixing bowl, combine the eggs and sugar and beat until pale yellow. Add the vanilla essence, nutmeg, lemon, salt, baking powder, and rice, and mix well. Add enough flour to bind the ingredients.

O In a deep frying pan or wok heat 3 inches oil to 365°F. (Remember that when oil gets above 350°F, the temperature can shoot up rapidly.) Drop teaspoonfuls of the batter into the oil, but do not crowd.

O Fry until golden, turning once, about 4 minutes. Remove, drain briefly, place on paper towels, and keep warm. Make sure the oil returns to 365°F before frying the next batch.

O Sift powdered sugar over the calas, or put the sugar in a bag, add a few calas at a time, and shake.

Scandinavian Rice and Almond Dessert

o o o

In the early 1800s rice was imported, so it was very expensive and reserved for special occasions only. Tradition demands that a bowl is put out for Santa Claus on Christmas Eve.

SERVES 8–10

3¾ cups milk
¼ cup sugar
1 cup long-grain white
  rice
scant ½ cup blanched
  almonds, halved

1 small wine glass of
  sherry
1–2 tsp vanilla essence
1 cup heavy cream,
  chilled

O Bring the milk to the boil. Add the sugar and rice, stirring occasionally. Lower the heat and simmer, uncovered, for about 25 minutes or until the rice is cooked. (To test, run a grain of rice between your thumb and forefinger; if there is no hard kernel in the center then the rice is done.) Pour the rice immediately into a shallow bowl to cool it quickly.

O When cool, add the almonds, sherry, and vanilla essence. Whip the cream in a chilled bowl until it thickens and holds it shape. Fold in the rice mixture. Turn into a serving dish and chill. A cold sherry or raspberry sauce is often served on top.

RIGHT *Calas*

116

Rice Soufflé

○ ○ ○

SERVES 4–6

½ cup short-grain rice	*4 eggs, separated*
⅓ cup sugar	*1 vanilla pod or a few*
¼ cup butter	*drops of vanilla*
3¾ cups milk	*essence*

SAUCE

½ pt puréed fruit	*2 tbsp water*
2 tsp cornstarch	

○ Rinse the rice well several times in cold water and allow to drain in the sieve.

○ Sprinkle the rice into a pan of hot water. Bring to the boil and cook for 3 minutes. Drain, and pour boiling water from the kettle over the grains.

○ Add the sugar and half the butter to most of the milk, keeping some to mix with the egg yolks. Add the vanilla pod at this stage, but if you are using vanilla essence add it at the end of the cooking. Heat the mixture, and add the rice. Cook until tender for about 30 minutes. After 15 minutes, add a little of the hot rice to the egg yolks and milk, and then return to the rice. Stir well for the remainder of the cooking time. Allow to cool slightly.

○ Butter a 7-inch soufflé dish. Preheat the oven to 375°F. Pour ½ inch water in the bottom of a roasting pan.

○ Whip up the egg whites to a fluffy consistency, but do not over-beat. Fold the vanilla essence and egg whites in the rice mixture, and turn into a soufflé dish standing in the water. Cook at 375°F for 25–30 minutes.

○ For a sauce any puréed fruit or fruit juice will do. Mix the cornstarch with the water, and add to the puréed fruit. Heat over a low heat until slightly thickened.

○ This soufflé should be served straight from the oven.

Creamy Chilled Rice

○ ○ ○

This dessert is served in the deep south of Spain for spoiling invalids and children, and it was taken to Paris by Eugenia de Montijo, to become *riz à l'impératrice*. It is normally dusted with cinnamon, but can be decorated with mandarin segments or grapes.

SERVES 6

⅓ cup short-grain rice	*powdered cinnamon*
5 cups milk	*2 lemons*
vanilla pod, split in 2	*1 cup heavy or*
generous 1 cup sugar	*whipping cream*
6 egg yolks	

○ Wash the rice in a sieve under running water. Tip it into a pan of boiling water and cook for 5 minutes, then drain well.

○ Heat 2 cups of milk in a pan and add the rice, half the vanilla pod, and 4 tbsp sugar. Simmer until the rice has expanded and the mixture is thick (25 minutes or so). Cream the egg yolks with the remaining sugar in a heatproof bowl that fits over a pan of simmering water. Heat the remaining milk and pour it into the egg and sugar mixture, adding the rest of the vanilla pod. Cook gently, stirring, until the custard coats the back of a spoon. Remove the vanilla pod. Stir the rice into the custard with just a pinch of cinnamon, and then leave until cold.

○ Cut 6 round disks of peel from the side of the lemons. Blanch them in boiling water for 2 minutes, then drain and refresh them under the cold faucet. Whip the cream, and fold into the rice. Turn into a shallow bowl, and push the lemon peel into the rice at regular intervals. Chill well. Before serving, dust cinnamon over the top.

Imperial Rice Mold with Kiwi Fruit

○ ○ ○

Serves 6

⅓ cup short-grain rice
⅓ cup sugar
½ cup candied fruit
2½ cups milk
3 egg yolks
1 tbsp gelatine powder
2 tbsp water

1¼ cups whipping
  cream
2 tsp Kirsch
a few drops of vanilla
¼ cup redcurrant jelly
2 kiwi fruit, peeled and
  sliced

○ Wash the rice and drain. Mix with the sugar and candied fruit in a saucepan. Pour in 2 cups milk, then allow to stand for at least 30 minutes.

○ Mix the egg yolks with the remaining milk.

○ Cook the rice in a saucepan, uncovered, by bringing the milk almost to the boil and then stirring over a low heat for about 15 minutes, or until the rice is tender. Add the egg yolks and milk for the last few minutes of cooking. Allow to cool.

○ Make up the gelatine by sprinkling the powder into 2 tbsp boiling water. It should dissolve, but if the water has cooled too much stand the heatproof container in boiling water for a few minutes to make sure.

○ Whip the cream lightly. Flavor with the Kirsch.

○ Wet a mold. Place in the refrigerator to chill.

○ Stir the gelatine into the cooled rice with the vanilla and, lastly, fold in the whipped cream. Pour into the mold and leave to set.

○ Warm the redcurrant jelly. Unmold the rice onto a serving plate, and run the slightly warmed jelly over the top.

○ Decorate with the kiwi fruit.

Pineapple Fruit Flan

○ ○ ○

SERVES 4

PASTRY

1½ cups flour	2 tbsp shortening
a pinch of salt	1 egg, separated
¼ cup hard margarine or butter	2–3 tbsp water

FILLING

¼ cup ground rice	½ tsp cinnamon
1¼ cups milk	1 egg yolk
2 tbsp butter	2 egg whites
grated rind of 1 lemon	1 tbsp sherry
juice of ½ lemon	about 10oz pineapple chunks
1 tsp sugar	

DECORATION

pieces of pineapple	6 candied cherries

○ To make the pastry, sieve the flour into a bowl and cut the fat into small, nut-sized pieces. Rub the fat in with the tips of the fingers. Mix with egg yolk and add a little water, using a round-bladed knife until a smooth consistency is obtained. Tip onto a lightly-floured board and knead lightly until smooth. Place in a refrigerator for at least 15 minutes.

○ Roll the pastry into a round about 1½ inches larger than the pie plate. Lift the pastry on a rolling pin and ease gently into the ring without stretching. Roll the top with the rolling pin and prick the bottom. Bake and cover with a piece of waxed paper weighted with baking beans for 15 minutes at 400°F.

○ Meanwhile make up the sauce for the filling by whisking the ground rice, milk, butter, grated lemon rind, a few drops of juice, sugar, and cinnamon over a low heat until thick. Allow to cool.

○ When the mixture is fairly cool beat in the egg yolk and sherry.

○ Chop or purée the fruit and line the bottom of the flan ring.

○ Whisk the egg whites until fluffy but do not overbeat, and fold into the rice mixture with a metal spoon. Tip into the flan ring and decorate with pieces of pineapple and cherries.

○ Bake in the oven at 350°F for 25 minutes.

Thai Sticky Rice with Mangoes

o o o

A simple dessert, but always successful. It works because of contrasts: in flavor between the sweetness of the coconut milk and the yellow Thai mango, and in texture between the rice and the mango.

SERVES 4–6

1lb rice
3½ cups thin coconut
   milk
¼ cup sugar

½ tsp salt
½ tsp cornstarch
2 ripe mangoes, peeled
   and sliced

O Soak the rice in water for 4 hours, rinse well 3 times in lukewarm water, and drain very well. Line a strainer with cheesecloth, add the rice, and place over a pan of boiling water — don't let the water touch the bottom of the rice. Cover and steam for about 30 minutes until fairly soft.

O Mix 3 cups of the coconut milk with the sugar and ¼ tsp of the salt. Stir in the rice and mix well.

O Mix the remaining coconut milk with the ¼ tsp salt and the cornstarch together in a small pan, bring to a boil, simmer for 2 minutes, and cool.

O Place the sticky rice onto serving plates, spoon the cornstarch sauce over the top, and arrange the mango slices around the edges.

Sweet Egg Cream

o o o

*T*his sweet egg cream is used as part of a number of Portuguese desserts and sweets, or may be served in small portions for a dessert. At Aveiro, on the Beira Litoral coast, it is traditionally sold in small wooden barrels or white shell-shaped containers. The use of the water from cooking rice is a fairly recent practice, but it improves the texture of the cream. The cream can be kept for 2–3 weeks in a covered container in the refrigerator.

SERVES 4–6

¼ cup short-grain rice
2 cups water

1 cup sugar
8 large egg yolks

O Simmer the rice in the water in a covered saucepan for about 30 minutes, until tender. Strain, and reserve ½ cup of the water. Discard the rice, or use it for another dish.

O Heat the sugar gently in the reserved rice water, stirring constantly, until the sugar has dissolved. Boil until reduced to a light syrup.

O Cool slightly and then slowly pour onto the egg yolks, whisking. Pour back into the pan in which the syrup was made and heat very gently, stirring, until thickened; do not allow it to boil as it will curdle.

O Use as required, or pour into a dish or individual dishes and leave to cool.

Apricot Rice Mold

o o o

SERVES 4–6

½ cup short-grain rice
½ cup sugar
⅓ cup butter
3¾ cups milk
4 eggs, separated

1 vanilla pod or a few
  drops of vanilla
  essence
⅔ cup whipping cream
1 tbsp gelatine powder
1lb canned apricots

O Wash the rice several times in a sieve, then drain.

O Add the sugar and butter to most of the milk in a saucepan. Retain ⅔ cup milk to mix with the egg yolks. Heat the milk, vanilla pod, butter, and sugar. If using vanilla essence, add at the end of cooking.

O Sprinkle the rice into the milk mixture, and stir over a low heat until the rice is cooked. Add a little of the hot rice mixture to the egg yolks and milk, and return to the saucepan for the last 5 minutes of cooking time. Allow to cool.

O Whip the cream lightly.

O Make up the gelatine by sprinkling it into ⅔ cup hot apricot juice in a heatproof cup. Stand the cup in boiling water and stir to completely dissolve the gelatine.

O Chop or blend half the apricot halves. Stir into the rice mixture with the gelatine. Allow to stand for 10 minutes.

O Whisk the egg whites until light and fluffy, but not to the hard peak stage.

O Fold the cream and vanilla essence into the rice mixture and, lastly, fold in the egg whites. Turn into a large mold or cake pan, and allow to set.

O Decorate with the remaining apricots.

Rice Eggs with Peach Sauce

o   o   o

SERVES 4

⅓ cup short-grain rice
¼ cup sugar
3 egg yolks
1¼ cups milk

½ tsp vanilla essence
1 tbsp golden raisins
1 tbsp mixed nuts,
    chopped

TO COAT

1 egg
⅔ cup dried
    breadcrumbs

TO FRY

4½ cups vegetable oil

PEACH SAUCE

1 small can of peaches

2 tsp arrowroot

O Wash the rice several times in cold water. Bring to the boil in a pan of water, and boil for 10 minutes. Drain into a sieve.

O Cook the rice and milk in a saucepan until the rice is soft. Use a double boiler if you prefer, otherwise stir over a low heat to prevent sticking.

O Add sugar and vanilla, and stir until the mixture leaves the sides of the pan. Turn out onto a plate. Chill.

O Divide into pieces about the size of a small egg, and roll on a floured board.

O Dip the croquettes in egg and breadcrumbs, and deep fry in the vegetable oil at 325°F until golden brown.

O To make the peach sauce, sieve or mash the fruit.

O Mix the arrowroot with a little cold water, and stir into the fruit mixture.

O Heat over a low heat until the sauce is thickened, and serve with the croquettes.

Mango and Kiwi Flowers

o o o

SERVES 4

2 ripe mangoes
2 ripe kiwi fruits

1lb (about 2–2½ cups) canned or homemade creamy rice pudding

RIGHT AND BELOW
Mango and Kiwi Flowers

○ Cut the mangoes in half. Remove the stones. Run a small, sharp knife in straight lines down each half, scoring the fruit without cutting the skin.

○ Turn the halved, marked fruit inside out carefully.

○ Peel the kiwi fruits and slice. Arrange the kiwi slices in between the mango cubes.

○ Divide the rice in 4 portions on serving plates, and top with the mango cubes.

Milk Pudding

o o o

*T*his baked milk pudding is made with ground rice.

SERVES 3–4

2½ cups milk
¼ cup ground rice
3 tbsp sugar

¼ tsp cinnamon
2 tbsp butter

○ Heat the milk in a saucepan without boiling.

○ Butter an ovenproof dish, which may have fruit or jam in the bottom, if preferred.

○ Sprinkle the ground rice into the milk, and continue stirring until the mixture comes to the boil and thickens. Remove from the heat.

○ Stir in the sugar and turn into the ovenproof dish; sprinkle with cinnamon and dot with butter. Bake for 25 minutes at 350°F.

Pineapple Rice Pudding

○ ○ ○

SERVES 4

2 tbsp butter
¼ cup short-grain rice
1¼ cups evaporated
  milk
1¼ cups water
3 tbsp sugar

½ tsp ground nutmeg
2 tbsp brown sugar
4 slices canned
  pineapple, drained
4 candied cherries

○ Butter an ovenproof pie dish well.

○ Wash the rice several times in a sieve with running cold water. Drain.

○ Pour the evaporated milk and water into the pie dish and sprinkle the rice on top. Add the sugar and stir well. If time allows, leave to stand in the refrigerator for 1–2 hours as this improves the pudding.

○ Sprinkle with nutmeg and add a few small pieces of butter to the surface.

○ Cover with loose foil to prevent a skin from forming and bake in the oven at 300°F for 30–40 minutes on a low shelf, then stir well to separate the grains. Continue cooking for a further 1–1¼ hours.

○ Remove the foil after 1¼ hours, and sprinkle with the brown sugar and arrange the pineapple rings on top. Return to the oven for a further 30–40 minutes.

○ Decorate with candied cherries in the center of each pineapple ring.

126

Shortbread

○ ○ ○

MAKES 2 CAKES

¾ cup flour
⅓ cup ground rice
1 cup butter

½ cup sugar
a pinch of salt

○ Sieve the flour and ground rice into a bowl.

○ Making sure the butter is fairly soft, place it in another bowl and add the sugar. Squeeze the sugar and butter together by hand so they mix well, but it is not necessary to cream the mixture.

○ Add the salt to the flour, and then gradually work in the lump of butter and sugar until a smooth ball is formed.

○ Turn out onto a floured surface (using a mixture of ground rice and flour). Knead until smooth. Roll out

2 balls, shape in a thistle or decorated mold, and turn onto a baking sheet. If a shortbread mold is not available, cook 2 cakes in 6-inch flan rings or sandwich pans. Mark the edges.

○ Cook in the oven for 1 hour at 325°F.

○ Sprinkle with sugar when cooling.

○ This mixture may be rolled out and cut into cookie shapes, which will only take 20 minutes to cook.

○ Alternatively, to make a delicious fruit shortcake, roll the mixture into an oblong about ½ inch thick. Cut off one oblong 7 inches long and 3 inches wide. Use this oblong as a base and cut the one left over into triangles. Once the shortbread pieces have been cooked, spread whipped cream on the base, cover it with fruit, and decorate it with the wedge shapes. Any suitable fruit can be used for decoration.

Index

o o o